Reproducible Activities

Reading Comprehension

Grades 7-8

Instructional Fair
An imprint of Carson-Dellosa Publishing, LLC
Greensboro, North Carolina

Instructional Fair

Editors: Kathryn Wheeler, Bruce Walker

Instructional Fair
An imprint of Carson-Dellosa Publishing, LLC
PO Box 35665
Greensboro, NC 27425 USA

ISBN 978-0-7424-1769-4
04-119138091

Table of Contents

Life in Yakutia

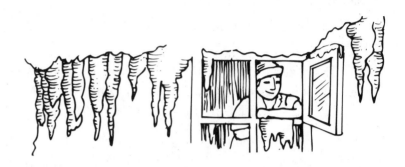

Many people who live in colder climates look forward to spring. Even if we embrace winter with all of its seasonal pleasures—skiing, ice hockey, and skating—we look forward to the day in March when the snow starts to disappear. So imagine a place that is so cold that a temperature just above freezing is considered a warm day. Imagine living in a place where your breath actually turns to ice the moment you step outside.

A place like this exists in a region of Russia called Yakutia. Located in the eastern part of Russia known as Siberia, it is one of the coldest areas in the world. In the town of Yakutsk, inhabitants have stated that it gets so cold that a corridor forms in the shape of a silhouette when a person walks down the street. The person's body heat actually cuts a path through the icy air, a path that others can see. After a person has passed out of sight, the corridor remains, hanging in the bright, cold air.

Some parts of Siberia receive between 30 and 50 inches (76–127 cm) of snow each year. But Yakutia has very little precipitation. You might think this is a good thing, but as a result, the region lacks the natural insulation that snow provides. The Yakutians layer the snow that does fall over their houses to form icy coatings to retain the heat. A traditional Yakutian house is a one-story, rectangular cabin with a nearly flat roof. Made of logs, it is sealed with mud, which also acts as insulation against the bitter cold.

Everything in Yakutia is built on *permafrost.* Permafrost is ground made up of ice and soil that stays frozen for most of the year. In fact, half of the land mass of the former Soviet Union rests on permafrost. Permafrost causes problems because it has an active layer that freezes in the winter and thaws during the summer. The thickness of this layer ranges from 3 to 10 feet (0.9–3 m). With the ground shifting so dramatically, it makes the construction of roads, buildings, pipelines, and other structures difficult. It's even difficult to dig graves in permafrost because of the instability of the ground. The Yakutians bury their dead in above-ground structures instead.

You might think that spring and summer would give the people of Yakutia a special sense of relief, but you would be wrong. Spring spells disaster for the inhabitants of this region. When the temperatures rise, their houses sink as the permafrost gives way. Sometimes only the roofs of houses can be seen from the street. Temperatures above freezing mean chaos in Yakutia. Mud oozes everywhere and tiny rivers of melted snow flood towns and settlements.

When winter returns, stability returns with it. The sub-zero temperatures put everything back in order. Houses, roads, and the ground itself stay glued together like the pieces of a model-train village. Paths and roads become passable again. In winter, life returns to normal.

Life in Yakutia (cont.)

Directions: Circle the correct answer.

1. What is the main idea of this article?

   A. Houses sometimes disappear in Yakutia.
   B. The people of Yakutia face special challenges because of the weather.
   C. Yakutia is located in Siberia, in eastern Russia.
   D. Spring is not the favorite season in Yakutia.

2. Which of these is a supporting detail from the story?

   A. Spring is a favorite time of year for many people because of the warmer weather.
   B. Life returns to normal at different times of the year in different places.
   C. The active layer of permafrost causes houses and roads in Yakutia to sink in the spring.
   D. The towns in Yakutia are like model-train villages.

3. Which supporting idea below is false?

   A. The weather in Yakutia is bitterly cold with many snowstorms.
   B. Yakutian houses are built with logs and sealed with mud to make them warm.
   C. It is so cold in Yakutia that a person's breath can freeze as soon as he steps outside.
   D. People in Yakutia use the snow that does fall to layer over their homes.

Directions: Match the vocabulary words to their meanings.

4. _____ corridor   A. material used to retain warmth

5. _____ insulation   B. a layer of mixed ice and soil

6. _____ permafrost   C. solidness; resistant to change

7. _____ stability   D. passage

8. _____ chaos   E. disorder or confusion

Directions: Write a response to each question. Be sure to use complete sentences.

9. Name another region of the world that faces special challenges because of the weather, and briefly describe those challenges.

   _____

   _____

10. Would you like to live in Yakutia? Why or why not?

    _____

    _____

The Indigo Highway

(1)Most people don't think of turtles as fast swimmers. How, then, do slow and clumsy loggerhead turtles wind up in Nova Scotia—thousands of miles from their Caribbean home? It isn't persistence that brings these turtles north. It's the Gulf Stream, a current that originates in the water south of Florida and ends up off the Grand Banks of Newfoundland, where it joins the North Atlantic current. The loggerhead turtles, along with giant blue fin tuna, blue sharks, and swordfish, hitch rides on this current, which moves faster than the ocean water around it.

(2)The Gulf Stream is like a giant river flowing within the ocean. It is between 50 and 100 miles wide (80.5 km–161 km) and about one mile (1.6 km) deep. But it moves much more water than any river on Earth—150 million cubic meters of water per second. That's 100 times the flow of all of the rivers in the world combined. It's not really possible to see the flow of this stream, but you can recognize it by its indigo, or deep blue, color. The Gulf Stream is also warmer than the northern Atlantic waters to its left and cooler than the Sargasso Sea to its right. In many ways, it acts as a barrier between these two sections of the Atlantic, deflecting the warmer water toward Europe.

(3)The Gulf Stream made its mark on history by affecting European travel to and from the New World. In 1519, Ponce de Léon's ship pilot, Antonio de Alaminos, discovered that sailing with the stream back to Europe saved a tremendous amount of time. This route became known as the "Highway of the Indies." Early sea captains who learned of it kept the directions a secret from competing traders.

(4)A century later, the Pilgrims had a very different experience with the Gulf Stream. It appears that they sailed against it, which is why their sea voyage took a lengthy 66 days. It may also explain how they ended up in Massachusetts instead of their original destination, Virginia. If they had crossed the Gulf Stream, it would have launched them north to New England.

(5)Benjamin Franklin showed a little more savvy when it came to understanding the ways of the Gulf Stream. While working in London just before the Revolutionary War, complaints reached him about the slowness of mail delivery from Great Britain to the colonies. He asked his cousin, a Nantucket whaling-ship captain, about this. His cousin told him that he and other whaling crews had seen British mail ships making slow progress while sailing in the Gulf Stream's current. The whaling ships, in contrast, used the stream to chase whales and make their capture possible. When the whaling ships tried to offer friendly advice to the mail ships, the British rejected the information and said they were "too wise to be counseled by simple American fishermen." Franklin continued to study the stream. Along with his cousin, he devised three amazingly accurate maps charting its course. Later, during his own voyages across the Atlantic, he followed the Gulf Stream's path by recording its warmer water temperatures with a thermometer.

(6)Oceanographers, amateur students of the sea, and others continue to take an interest in the Gulf Stream. Many features of this huge current remain a fascinating mystery. In the meantime, loggerhead turtles and other sea creatures happily take their free rides on the indigo highway of the ocean.

Name _____ Date _____

The Indigo Highway (cont.)

Directions: Fill in the chart. In Column 1, write the main idea of each paragraph. In Column 2, write two details from the paragraph that supports the main idea.

	Main Idea	**Supporting Details**
Paragraph 1	_____	1. The Gulf Stream starts in Florida. _____ 2. _____
Paragraph 2	_____	1. _____ 2. _____
Paragraph 3	_____	1. _____ 2. _____
Paragraph 4	The Gulf Stream made the Pilgrims' journey difficult.	1. _____ 2. _____
Paragraph 5	_____	1. _____

Dog Data

Do you consider a dog your best friend? Or did a bad experience with a dog make you wary of canines? Either way, it pays to know something about this species that has lived with humans for thousands of years. Some scientists who study animal behavior believe that dogs could be descended from wolves. Another theory is that dogs are the animal cousins of wolves, with dogs and wolves sharing a common ancestor. For this reason, the study of wolf behavior has proven to be helpful in understanding the actions of dogs.

Have you ever wondered why dogs bury bones? A look at the behavior of wolves tells us something about how canines handle food. Single wolves and small groups of wolves can eat some of their prey in one sitting— animals ranging in size from rabbits to sheep. In fact, one adult wolf can eat the equivalent of 176 quarter-pound hamburgers in a day! That might be where the expression "wolf down one's food" comes from. However, large prey such as cattle or caribou can be more meat than a small pack of wolves can consume. Rather than leave the surplus for vultures, the thrifty wolves bury their leftovers and dig them up the next day for another meal. Dogs follow this behavior when they bury bones. Even though a dog is fed every day, its instinct tells it to treat the bone as surplus food to be saved and savored again.

Why do dogs bark? Let's look to wolves again. Wolves bark to warn the members of the pack of a possible threat. A wolf's bark prompts the adults in the pack to hide their pups and prepare for action. The bark of a wolf is terse and relatively quiet. By contrast, a dog's bark can be noisy and prolonged. But the purpose of the barking is the same. Dogs' barks are warnings to their human family. The dog is saying, "I notice something unusual. Pay attention!" A barking dog is not necessarily getting ready to attack. The barking is simply telling others to be alert.

Whether dogs will attack an unwelcome stranger depends on the dog's breeding, training, and individual personality. Almost every dog, however, views its human owners as members of its pack. It considers the house in which it lives to be its den. Dogs, like wolves, are protective of their pack members and prefer to huddle together for security. That's why dogs like to sleep with their owners. Sharing a bed with a dog may be against the rules in some homes, but keeping the dog in the basement or in a kennel isn't wise either. In the wild, only outcast wolves sleep away from the pack, usually because they have been driven away. A dog that is forced to sleep in isolation will start to feel and act like an outcast. Human owners who find a way to let their dogs sleep as near to them as possible often have fewer problems with their pets.

Years of breeding and living in the world of humans have made dogs some of the best animal friends we have.

◆◆◆◆◆◆◆◆◆◆◆◆◆◆◆◆◆◆◆◆◆◆◆◆◆◆◆◆◆◆◆◆◆

Dog Data (cont.)

Directions: Circle the best answer.

1. Scientists believe that dogs and wolves—

    A. have nothing in common.

    B. could be animal cousins.

    C. may share a common ancestor.

    D. both B and C

2. What kind of scientific research on wolves has been a help in understanding the actions of dogs?

    A. life expectancy

    B. hunting habits

    C. behavior

    D. both A and B

3. For what reason do wolves bury leftover food?

    A. to save it for the next day

    B. to hide it from scavengers

    C. to fertilize the soil

    D. both A and B

4. The sound of a barking wolf is—

    A. quiet

    B. loud

    C. terse

    D. both A and C

5. How do dogs view their human owners?

    A. as pack members

    B. as enemies

    C. as outcasts

    D. both B and C

6. Why do some wolves sleep away from the pack?

    A. they don't like the pack

    B. they are outcasts

    C. the den is too crowded

    D. both B and C

Directions: Write an answer to the question. Be sure to use complete sentences.

7. Write the main idea of the article in one sentence. In two additional sentences, write two details that support the main idea.

_____

_____

_____

_____

_____

Mealtime Manners

What do you think your parents would say if, at your next Thanksgiving dinner, you took a handful of turkey from the platter and crammed it into your mouth? What if you then used the serving spoon to eat some dressing, and took your grandmother's glass of water and used it to wash down your mouthful? Of course, they would be horrified, but this style of eating would actually be true to tradition. The Pilgrims, celebrating their first Thanksgiving dinner with their Native American friends, probably ate in just such a manner.

Today, most people in Western cultures expect to eat meals with their own set of silverware, their own plate, and their own glass. Diners use the plates to hold their food and drink only from their own glasses. But Europeans did not always eat this way.

In the 1500s, members of the ruling classes used knives to carve helpings of meat. Since they rarely had their own plates and bowls, they would eat the slice of meat off the tip of the knife. They would use shared spoons to eat soup and would dip bread or their fingers into serving bowls of gravy or stew. If a person was rich enough to own a spoon or knife, he or she would carry these to a banquet and use them instead of their hands. There were a few rules for eating behavior. It was considered rude to taste something from a spoon if it was being passed down to another diner. If you had a bone left in your hand after eating a chicken leg, you were expected to toss it politely under the table.

The working poor had even fewer mealtime manners, since they were usually just worried about getting enough food each day to survive. Their main utensils were their hands. When Europeans, such as the Pilgrims, settled in the New World, they brought this eating style with them. They used pieces of bread as spoons for soup, used their fingers for other food, and passed a shared cup at meals.

While the colonists were sharing cups and dipping their fingers into bowls of food, European royalty and nobility were starting to expand their tableware. They were also developing manners to go with their new knives, forks, spoons, plates, and napkins. They started to think of sharing cups or platters as unsanitary and even rude. Their new manners set them apart and underscored their status as an upper class. By the 1700s, these new customs had spread to wealthy American settlers. As new landowners, they wanted to have a higher status than they would have had in Great Britain. They bought their own dishes and silverware and brought them to the colonies.

By the late 1800s, mealtime manners had changed for everyone. As the American middle class grew, so did their demand for tableware that showed off their prosperity. There was also an elaborate system of etiquette or manners by this time. This new emphasis on behavior extended to every aspect of everyday life, but was particularly important at meals.

And what about the 21st century? Do our manners continue to become more complex? Just the opposite seems true. We eat fresh fruit and raw vegetables by hand, along with cheese and crackers. We buy burgers and fries at a fast-food restaurant and eat them in the car. We use our hands to eat pizza and tacos. Mealtimes are becoming more casual all the time.

Mealtime Manners (cont.)

Directions: Circle the correct answer.

1. What is the main idea of this story?

   A. Thanksgiving dinner was eaten by hand.

   B. Manners for mealtimes have changed over time.

   C. We are eating more and more like our ancestors.

   D. Sharing cups and spoons was not rude in the 1500s.

2. Choose the supporting detail for this sentence: "There were a few rules for eating behavior in the 1500s."

   A. It was considered rude not to use a napkin.

   B. European royalty started to expand their tableware.

   C. You were supposed to toss any bones under the table.

   D. There was an elaborate system of etiquette for banquets.

3. Why did landowners in colonial America buy silverware and dishes?

   A. They wanted to eat more neatly and not spill as many things.

   B. They wanted to prove they had a higher status than they would have had in Great Britain.

   C. They wanted to become members of royalty.

   D. They wanted to have more sanitary eating conditions in their homes.

4. What is ironic about mealtime manners in the 21st century?

   A. After developing a system of table manners, we are starting to eat by hand again.

   B. We are starting to share cups and plates again.

   C. After importing a lot of dishes and silverware, we have worse manners.

   D. We are eating like the Pilgrims, even at Thanksgiving dinner.

Directions: Match the vocabulary words to their meanings.

5. _____ status   A. manners

6. _____ etiquette   B. silverware

7. _____ elaborate   C. unclean

8. _____ utensils   D. rank

9. _____ unsanitary   E. complicated or complex

Name _____ Date _____

Family Tree

"How did Grandma and Grandpa meet each other, Mom?" asked Sonia.

"I didn't know you were interested in that old stuff," her mother replied, smiling. "They met in 1936. They helped out on the same farm after school. Grandma didn't have many friends at the time."

"What were Grandma's mother and father named?" asked Sonia.

"Their names were Regina and Gerald Hellstern," said her mother. "Gerald was the first person in his whole family to be born outside of Germany. That was in 1885. His family had been in the United States for four years when he was born."

Sonia was impressed. "Wow, that was a long time ago. How do you know about all this?"

"For the past few years, your uncle and I have been researching our family history," her mother answered. "We have reconstructed a family tree that goes all the way back to 1749."

"A family tree? What kind of tree is that?" asked Sonia, getting a little confused.

"It's not a real tree, honey," was the answer. "Here, look at this."

Sonia watched her mother draw lines and write names on a piece of paper. She told Sonia a few stories about her ancestors: how her great-uncle had fought in World War I, how her great-grandmother learned English from a neighbor, and how her grandfather had started his business. Sonia was amazed at how interesting their lives were.

"Please tell me more," Sonia pleaded.

Name _____ Date _____

Family Tree (cont.)

Directions: Circle the correct answer.

1. From what country were some of Sonia's ancestors?

   A. Mexico

   B. Poland

   C. Germany

   D. England

2. Sonia's great-grandfather was the first person in his family to—

   A. leave Germany.

   B. be born in Germany.

   C. be born outside of Germany.

   D. work on a farm after school.

3. Why hadn't Sonia's mother told her family stories before?

   A. Family histories are only for adults.

   B. She thought that the stories were too sad to tell.

   C. She thought that Sonia was too young to hear the stories.

   D. She did not know that Sonia would be interested.

4. Sonia probably will—

   A. ask to hear more stories about her ancestors.

   B. quickly grow tired of the family stories.

   C. write a letter to her grandparents.

   D. ask a friend to tell her family stories.

5. Which statement about Sonia is supported by the text?

   A. She is not interested in past events.

   B. She likes to hear made-up stories.

   C. She is mainly interested in herself.

   D. She seems to like learning about new things.

6. What is the main idea of this story?

   A. A girl learns about her ancestors for the first time.

   B. A girl has just moved to the United States from Germany.

   C. A girl works on a farm along with her mother.

   D. A girl helps her mother research their family tree.

Directions: Write an answer to the question. Be sure to use complete sentences.

7. Write a fact that you know about someone in your family.

   _____

   _____

   _____

   _____

Pirates

The year is 1720. After living on a Caribbean plantation for most of your 14 years, you are sailing to Spain. There are rumors that the British are going to take over your family's island home, and your parents have sent you away because they want you to be safe.

The large galleon on which you are traveling is loaded down with valuable furniture, jewelry, gold coins, and bars of silver. Just as your ship rounds Haiti, you notice another ship turning toward you. With a gasp, you strain to see the ship's flag—the main way of distinguishing friends from enemies on the sea. With relief, you see that the flag is black and features a skull above two crossed swords. Relief? Yes, the ship is manned by pirates, but a black flag is better news than a red flag would have been. The black flag means that if the captain of the ship cooperates with the pirates, they might spare the lives of those on board. A red flag would have meant no *quarter*, or mercy. After killing most of the people on board, they might have spared your young life, but taken you to work on their pirate ship.

The pirates who sailed in the 1600s and 1700s are not like the ones seen in today's movies. Although real-life pirates did rob and plunder, not all of them were merciless cutthroats. Captain Tew, for example, was known for his kind treatment of prisoners. Because of this, many ships surrendered to him without any fight at all. Another pirate, the mild-mannered Captain Misson of France, started a retirement home for old and disabled pirates.

But some pirates were feared for good reason. Stede Bonnet started out life in luxury with a wealthy wife and four children. But when he tired of domestic life, he abandoned his family and joined forces with Blackbeard. Bonnet was probably the only pirate who actually forced his prisoners to walk the plank. Blackbeard was equally ferocious. He was known to shoot at his crew members just to scare them. His appearance alone was terrifying. He had a huge nose, bloodshot eyes, and an immense black beard.

Captain Kidd is a name that most people equate with piracy. He was actually a respected New York merchant with a family. Like many pirates, he began working as a *privateer*, a captain who was allowed by the government to attack the ships of enemy countries on the high seas. Pressured into the job by the British, he was supposed to attack only French ships. But his crew overtook his ship and attacked Moorish and British ships as well. The British hung Kidd for these crimes, and he died as a scapegoat for the acts of genuine pirates who eluded capture.

Let's get back to you and that approaching pirate ship. The crossed swords instead of bones mark the flag as belonging to Calico Jack Rackham. As Calico Jack and his crew board your ship, you are startled to see that two of the pirates are women. They are Anne Bonney and Mary Read. These two pirates have a reputation for being absolutely fearless in battle. You hope that your captain has the good sense to cooperate!

Pirates (cont.)

Directions: Match each story detail to information about it.

1. _____ black flag
2. _____ red flag
3. _____ Calico Jack Rackham
4. _____ Anne Bonney
5. _____ Stede Bonnet
6. _____ privateer

A. flew a flag with a skull and crossed swords

B. was a fearless female pirate

C. means "no quarter given"

D. a captain allowed to attack enemy ships

E. means "mercy for cooperation"

F. made his victims walk the plank

Directions: Write the correct answer.

7. The story says that Captain Kidd died "as a scapegoat." What does that mean?

   _____

   _____

8. Write the main idea of this story in one complete sentence.

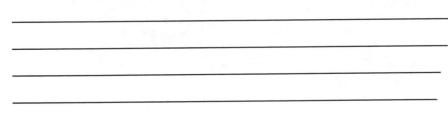

Mathew Brady's Career

Mathew Brady tried to end warfare for all time. He used a new, powerful weapon. He used a camera.

Brady opened his first photography studio in 1844. The images he produced were *daguerreotypes*, not the photographs he would take later. Daguerreotypes recorded images on sheets of copper coated with silver. They required long exposures, so the person being photographed would have to stay perfectly still for three to 15 minutes. That made daguerreotypes impractical for portraits. By 1855, Brady was advertising a new type of image that had just been invented: a photograph made on paper.

From the beginning of his career, Brady believed that photography could serve an important purpose. His images could create a record of national life. When the Civil War broke out, he wanted to document the war as a part of that record. His friends discouraged him, but Brady started to take photographs of war scenes. He assembled a corps of photographers who worked in the field, taking photographs of battle scenes and military

life. He also bought photographs from others who were returning from the field. His efforts culminated in an 1862 display of photographs made after the Battle of Antietam. The bloodshed shocked the visitors to the exhibit, most of whom had never seen a field of battle.

Brady did not stop warfare with his work, but he did raise the awareness of the costs of war among common citizens. After the Civil War, people lost interest in his chronicle of the war. Because he could find few buyers for his photographs and did not earn enough money to pay for his wartime work, Brady went bankrupt. Years after the war, Congress bought Brady's collection. It is now considered a priceless documentation of the War between the States. Other photographs by Mathew Brady sell for thousands of dollars and are considered national treasures.

Mathew Brady's Career (cont.)

Directions: Circle the correct answer.

1. Which sentence best summarizes this entire story?

   A. Mathew Brady went bankrupt, but now his photographs are valuable.

   B. Mathew Brady wanted to use photography to create a record of national life.

   C. Mathew Brady first took daguerreotypes, but switched to photographs.

   D. Mathew Brady was the first photographer in the United States.

2. Which sentence best summarizes the final paragraph of the story?

   A. Mathew Brady went bankrupt, but now his photographs are considered valuable.

   B. Mathew Brady helped to stop warfare in the United States.

   C. Mathew Brady's photographs of the Civil War were bought by Congress.

   D. Mathew Brady's work is not treasured today.

3. How did Mathew Brady chronicle the Civil War?

   A. He took photographs of wartime scenes.

   B. He assembled a group of photographers to take pictures of the war.

   C. He bought pictures from other photographers who were returning from the field.

   D. All of the above

4. Which sentence summarizes Brady's wartime efforts?

   A. His work shocked people so much that they did not want to see him.

   B. His work shocked people but raised their awareness of the costs of war.

   C. His work shocked most people but not members of Congress.

   D. His work is not considered valuable today.

Directions: Write a response to each question.

5. Why do you think people were so shocked by Brady's photographs?

   _____

   _____

   _____

6. What do you consider most important about Brady's career?

   _____

   _____

   _____

7. Summarize in one sentence how you think photography has changed the world.

   _____

   _____

   _____

Alex in Charge

Alex was thrilled. Finally, she was being allowed to babysit her sister Connie all by herself. Connie was four, and their mother called her "a little handful." But Alex knew that she would be able to handle Connie and become a great babysitter.

After their parents left, Alex and Connie sat down to watch TV. "We're going to watch my show, because I'm in charge," announced Alex. Connie burst into tears. She got up, stood right in front of the TV screen, and refused to move. Alex had to drag her to one side, and Connie kicked and screamed. "You sit here because I say so!" Alex shouted. Connie lay down on the floor and sobbed.

Alex couldn't even hear the TV, so she finally turned it off. "Okay, now we are going to play a game," said Alex. Connie sniffed but sat up and listened. "I'll pick words and we can both try to spell them," said Alex. "The winner gets dessert and the loser doesn't." Since Connie couldn't read yet, she lost the game, although she did try to spell some words. Tears rolled down her cheeks when Alex announced that she would get no dessert that evening.

"Time for dinner!" said Alex. She microwaved her favorite meal, macaroni and cheese. "We are having this because I'm in charge," she said to Connie, who hated macaroni and cheese. Connie took her bowl and dumped it on the floor—upside down.

"You did that on purpose!" said Alex. "You are going to bed right now because I am in charge!" She carried a screaming Connie under her arm as she trudged up the stairs.

Suddenly, Connie stopped crying. "What was that?" she asked in a small, scared voice. Alex stopped and listened. It sounded as if someone was climbing up the side of the house! Then they heard a knocking at the hall window.

Alex and Connie held onto each other. "You stay here on the stairs," Alex whispered. "I am going to look." She crept around the corner and crawled to the hall window. She moved the curtain with a shaking hand. It was a broken tree branch, tapping against the windowpane! Alex ran back, picked up Connie, and carried her to the window to show her. Then they both fell onto Connie's bed, exhausted.

When their parents came home, they found Alex and Connie asleep, with Alex's arm around her younger sister. "Isn't wonderful to see how well the girls get along?" Mom said, smiling.

Alex in Charge (cont.)

Directions: Write **T** for true or **F** for false.

1. _____ This is a good summary of the story: Alex turns out to be a great babysitter the first time she tries.

2. _____ This is a good summary of Alex's character: She is bossy but brave.

3. _____ This is a good summary of Connie's character: She is quiet and obedient.

4. _____ Alex keeps repeating that she is in charge because she wants Connie to relax and have fun.

5. _____ Another title for this story might be "The Best Babysitter Ever."

6. _____ Connie turns out to be a good babysitter after all.

7. Sum up in a sentence why you think Alex behaves the way she does in the story.

   _____

   _____

   _____

8. Why is the ending of the story ironic?

   _____

   _____

   _____

   _____

The Irish Famine

On May 1, 1848, the *Swan* set sail from Cork, Ireland. The ship carried victims of the Irish famine to a new life in North America.

The passengers watched as Ireland disappeared on the horizon behind them. They were leaving their home forever. But they were also leaving the horrors of the past few years. Fields lay black with rot and relatives died of starvation and disease. Their trials were not over when they boarded the ship, however. Ahead stretched a dangerous voyage. On ships transporting these Irish citizens, cholera and other diseases passed from one person to the next, infecting everyone and often killing up to one-third of the passengers. The newspapers of the time called the emigration ships "coffin ships" because of the high death rate aboard them.

It was a single crop that started the problem, a crop on which the poor of Ireland were too dependent: the potato. Through generations, Irish parents and their grown children divided farms into smaller and smaller lots. Grain could not be grown on these small plots of land, but potatoes could. Poor Irish families depended almost entirely on this plant for food, and grew the same varieties year after year. When the plant virus known as the potato

blight was accidentally introduced into the country in 1845, it spread quickly throughout the country. Year after year, the crops died. So did the Irish people. So many people died that relatives could not buy coffins, even if they had the money to do so. Entire families and whole villages were wiped out. It was the worst European famine of the 19th century.

The famine changed Ireland in many ways. After the famine ended, farmers tried new methods and new crops to avoid the tragedy of the past. The Irish people varied their diet. They mourned the people they had lost through death and emigration to North America. In 1844, Ireland's population was over eight million people. By 1851, more than a million were dead, and a million and a half more had emigrated to North America. The lowly potato had changed a country and its people forever.

Name _____ Date _____

The Irish Famine (cont.)

Directions: Match the two parts of each sentence. Then use this information to write a summary of the article.

1. ____ The Irish Famine occurred

2. ____ The crops of the Irish people

3. ____ Whole villages were

4. ____ It was the worst European famine

5. ____ By the end of the famine, the population of Ireland

6. ____ After the famine,

A. wiped out from starvation.

B. between 1845 and 1851.

C. of the 19th century.

D. was reduced by two and a half million.

E. were killed by potato blight.

F. farmers varied their crops and methods.

7. Write your summary of the story.

_____

_____

_____

_____

_____

_____

_____

_____

_____

_____

_____

Mummies Have No Secrets

Mummies cannot hide their age. They cannot hide what they ate for their last meals or whether their families were wealthy or poor. Mummies, in fact, cannot hide much of anything from the anthropologists who study them.

The wrappings on a mummy and the artifacts found with the body reveal much about the social status of the person. For example, a mummy found in the Taklimakan Desert sported a bronze earring and leather boots. The decorations on these items showed that the mummy's people were skilled artisans. Other items found in the tombs of mummies include statues and jewelry, or sometimes tools that the person might have used in life as a craftsperson.

A mummy's body reveals even more clues. The contents of a mummy's digestive tract can be examined both chemically and microscopically, offering clues about the person's diet. When anthropologists studied the Iceman, a mummy found in Italy, they examined the contents of his intestines.

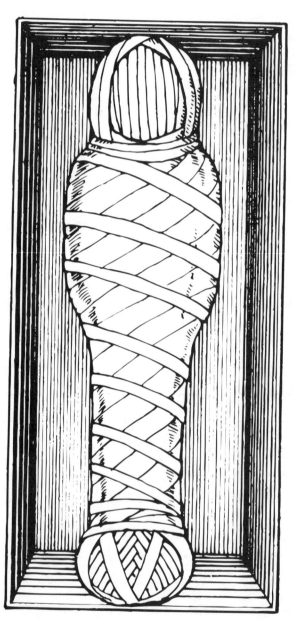

They wanted to see what he ate in the hours before his death.

Organs and bones reveal details about the way the person died, too. Even if no flesh remains, bones and teeth can reveal the age of the person at death, as well as more details about diet, height, occupation, ethnicity, and social status. For example, a male mummy's worn front teeth might indicate that he used his teeth to hold a tool, freeing his hands for other work. In addition, since bone absorbs minerals during a person's life, a chemical study of the bones turns up information about the diet of the deceased person. If DNA can be extracted from the mummy, scientists can even determine the mummy's blood type.

Even death and 5,000 years of burial cannot hide a mummy's secrets. These secrets help contribute to what we know about ancient life and culture.

Mummies Have No Secrets (cont.)

Directions: Circle **Yes** or **No**.

1. Unless flesh remains on a mummy, scientists can tell little about it.
    Yes   No

2. One possible source of information about mummies is from DNA.
    Yes   No

3. Three sources of study from mummies are wrappings, teeth, and artifacts.
    Yes   No

4. The mummy known as the Iceman wore a bronze earring.
    Yes   No

5. A mummy's bones can be studied chemically.
    Yes   No

6. Mummies are studied so that we can know more about ancient life.
    Yes   No

7. Write a summary of the article "Mummies Have No Secrets." In your summary, explain the meaning of the story's title.

    _____

    _____

    _____

    _____

    _____

Canoes

Canoes have been around for hundreds of years and have been made in all shapes and sizes. Generally, a canoe is thought of as a boat that is pointed at both ends with a relatively flat bottom. It is wider in the middle than at the ends. This makes it buoyant enough to be used in shallow water and stable enough to be used in deep water. Canoes are usually propelled by paddles, but some can also be sailed.

The name *canoe* comes from the Spanish version of an Arawak word, *canao*. The Arawaks were people who lived on islands in the Caribbean. They made their canoes, known as *dugouts*, from whole pieces of trees. They chose a tree that was the right length for a canoe, cut it down, trimmed off all the branches, and hauled it close to the water's edge. While removing the bark, they scraped an outline of the area they would hollow out to create the interior of the canoe. Then they dumped hot coals on this outlined spot to burn out a cockpit. Dippers of water were used to control the fire. The burning also dried the sap from the log, making the boat waterproof. Then the Arawaks carved the ends into points to help the boat glide through the water. This dugout would be paddled by two people, both of whom steered.

A *kayak* is another form of a canoe. The kayak was developed by the Inuits, natives of Greenland, the Arctic Circle, and the Hudson

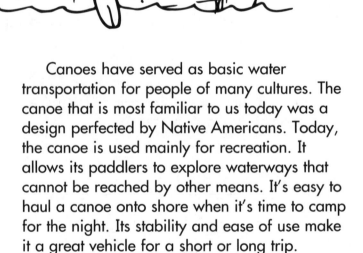

Bay coasts of North America. These natives made kayaks by constructing frames of driftwood or animal bones, which they bound together with gut. The frame was covered completely in sealskin, except for a hole at the top that created the cockpit. The sealskin, which was sewn onto the frame, was naturally waterproof. A kayak is paddled by only one person, who has to steer by him- or herself.

Canoes have served as basic water transportation for people of many cultures. The canoe that is most familiar to us today was a design perfected by Native Americans. Today, the canoe is used mainly for recreation. It allows its paddlers to explore waterways that cannot be reached by other means. It's easy to haul a canoe onto shore when it's time to camp for the night. Its stability and ease of use make it a great vehicle for a short or long trip.

Canoes (cont.)

Directions: Use the phrases in the box to fill in the Venn diagram.

made from a wood or bone frame	paddled by two people	used by the Arawak
types of canoes	paddled by one person	made from a tree
burned to make	waterproof	stable water transportation
	used by the Inuit	

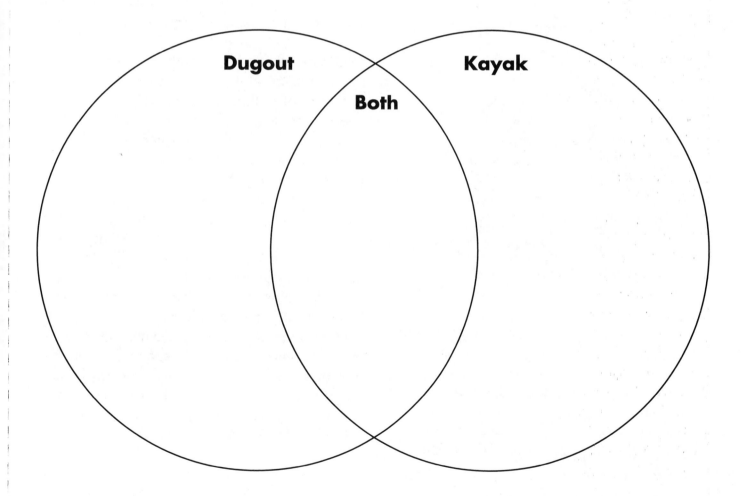

Dugout   **Kayak**

Both

Vampires?

A man wandered in the dark night. During the day, he shrank from strong light. He avoided mirrors. He bared his teeth when approached by others or when he smelled garlic. When he died, horrified villages reported that his body still looked lifelike.

This true account from the 7th century sounds like something from a Hollywood horror film. But Spanish neurologist Juan Gomez-Alonso has a better explanation. The man in the report was probably the victim of rabies. The symptoms are remarkably similar to untreated rabies cases, the doctor notes.

Legends about vampires first spread through Europe in the late 1600s. Since that time, books and movies have embroidered these myths. Supposedly, vampires drink blood. Most vampires are portrayed as male. They have pale skin and staring eyes. They sleep during the day and wander at night. They can be warded off with garlic or mirrors. They are difficult to kill and can rise up even when people think they are dead.

Gomez-Alonso noticed that these kinds of vampire myths began circulating in Eastern Europe and Russia at about the same time that a rabies epidemic swept through the area. Another epidemic of rabies hit Hungary between 1721 and 1728, and suddenly stories of vampires were being published there. The doctor's research has correlated other incidents as well.

Here are some facts: More than seven times as many men as women contract rabies. Early symptoms include irritability and sleeplessness. As the disease progresses without treatment, some people will bite or attack others. About 25 percent of people infected with rabies will also bite other rabies victims. Strong light, reflections from mirrors, and strong odors will trigger spasms that seem to change the faces of sufferers. Also, throat spasms will make rabid people bare their teeth and froth at the mouth. During such a spasm, a person may bite his tongue or the inside of his cheek and the froth will have blood in it.

Even in death, the disease of rabies changes normal human body responses. The illness makes the blood stay liquid longer. This keeps the skin looking pink and lifelike for longer than normal.

Because this disease was untreatable for hundreds of years and ran its course with the full range of symptoms, Gomez-Alonso concluded that "vampires" were actually victims of rabies. As people had to face the terrifying range of symptoms, they constructed their own stories to explain the dramatic changes in behavior of the disease's victims.

Vampires? (cont.)

Directions: Fill in the chart to compare the "vampires" of legends to real-life sufferers of rabies.

	Vampires	**Rabies Victims**
Gender	_____	_____
Appearance	_____	_____
	_____	_____
	_____	_____
Behavior	_____	_____
	_____	_____
	_____	_____
Death	_____	_____
	_____	_____
	_____	_____

At Sheila's House

"I'm starving," said Kelly as she and Sheila walked home from school.

Sheila sighed. "You're always starving," she said. "We'll have something when we get to my house."

Kelly looked at Sheila, who was walking quickly down the sidewalk. Sheila had long, beautiful red hair and always wore perfect outfits. Kelly had short hair and many of her clothes were hand-me-downs.

No one was home when they got to Sheila's house. No one ever seemed to be home at Sheila's house. Kelly had two sisters and a brother. "It must be amazing to have the whole house to yourself. I'm lucky if I can be alone for five minutes," said Kelly.

"It's awesome," Sheila replied. "I can do whatever I want. Do you want to order a pizza? There's nothing in the refrigerator." There was never anything in Sheila's refrigerator.

"That's okay," said Kelly. "I have to go home for dinner soon."

Sheila rolled her eyes. "I would go crazy if people were telling me what to do all the time."

"Well, you're lucky," said Kelly. Sheila was lucky. She had perfect hair, perfect clothes, a perfect house. "I would give anything to be Sheila for just one day," thought Kelly.

The phone rang. "Hi, Mom," Kelly heard Sheila say. "No, it's okay. I understand." She hung up. "My mom's having dinner out again," she said. "Are you sure you can't stay for pizza?"

"Sorry. I have to go or I'll be late for dinner," said Kelly.

"Whatever. See you."

Kelly saw Sheila looking out the window as she walked down the street. Suddenly, Sheila's house looked very big, and Sheila looked very small.

At Sheila's House (cont.)

Directions: Circle the correct answer.

1. Which of these is the best contrast between Sheila's life and Kelly's?

   A. Sheila is from a big family and Kelly is from a small one.

   B. Kelly has a big, caring family and Sheila is often on her own.

   C. Kelly has perfect clothes and Sheila wears hand-me-downs.

   D. Sheila and Kelly have similar family situations.

2. Which of these contrasts is true?

   A. Kelly has brothers and sisters; Sheila is an only child.

   B. Sheila's mother does not have much money; Kelly's parents are wealthy.

   C. Kelly is a good student; Sheila is a struggling student.

   D. Kelly lives in a big house; Sheila lives in a smaller house.

3. Which things about Sheila's life does Kelly envy?

   A. her house, her parents, and her clothes

   B. her hair, her clothes, and her pets

   C. her hair, her clothes, and her house

   D. her clothes, her parents, and her pets

4. What things about Kelly's life might Sheila envy?

   A. the fact that Kelly has sisters to loan her clothes

   B. the fact that Kelly has caring parents who are there to take care of her

   C. the fact that Kelly has a big house and lots of time to herself

   D. the fact that Kelly gets to eat pizza almost every night of the week

5. Why do you think the author includes the final sentence of the story?

   A. to show that Sheila lives in a big, beautiful house

   B. to show that Sheila gets to do whatever she wants

   C. to show that Sheila is spoiled

   D. to show that Sheila is lonely

Directions: Write an answer to the question. Be sure to use complete sentences.

6. Would you rather have a life more like Kelly's or Sheila's? Explain why.

   _____

   _____

   _____

   _____

   _____

Prairie Pioneers

In some of the most remote, least-populated places in the prairie, there are bustling towns that have existed for centuries. The founders of these towns built intricate systems of underground tunnels. The present-day inhabitants still use these tunnels; some are the descendants of the original pioneers and some are newer residents. On the fringes of these towns, enemies of the citizens lurk; sometimes they make sneak attacks on the downtown dwellers.

These are the towns of the black-tailed prairie dogs, who have one of the tightest-knit communities in the animal kingdom. These fascinating and often misunderstood animals are worth a closer look.

First, prairie dogs are not even distantly related to domestic dogs. They get their name from their barking, which is how they communicate with each other and warn of intruders. Prairie dogs are actually sleek, plump members of the squirrel family. A prairie dog has small, rounded ears; a long, thin tail; short legs; and a yellow-gray or tawny coat.

Prairie dogs live on what is left of the great American prairie, which extends from Canada to northern Mexico. Prairie dogs were once viewed as a problem. Because they eat grass and herbs, just like cattle, ranchers viewed prairie dogs as a threat to their cattle. On their own and with government agencies, ranchers mounted massive campaigns to poison and shoot prairie dogs. As a result, the prairie dog population was reduced by 90 percent in the United States. Some breeds of prairie dogs now are considered threatened or endangered.

But there are still black-tailed prairie dogs plowing through the dirt, expanding their underground towns. Some of these towns extend for several miles and are home to thousands of prairie dogs. Like human cities, these towns are divided into wards, and are assigned to several extended families or *coteries*. Prairie dogs will defend their wards against all strangers, including other prairie dogs. Family members greet each other by a gesture that looks like kissing; they are really checking each other's scent. They also show affection by playing together and grooming each other. Young prairie dogs actually play versions of tag and hide-and-seek with each other.

When a prairie dog sees danger, usually in the form of a bird of prey, a coyote, or a badger, it stands on its hind legs and gives a shrill warning bark. Other prairie dogs dive underground as soon as the warning is given. The opening shafts that lead to the underground city plunge down between 10 and 12 feet (between 3 and 3.7 m). When prairie dogs dig new tunnels, they use the dirt to construct crater-shaped cones around the entrances. These barriers keep out water. The wards include networks of tunnels, including *turning bays* (for turning around) and apartment-like chambers.

If you're ever driving through the prairie and you think the rolling expanse of land is boring, just think of the thriving city that might lie just below the grass.

Prairie Pioneers (cont.)

Directions: Use the information from the story, along with your knowledge of domestic dogs, to fill in the chart. Then compare these two kinds of animals.

Category	Prairie Dogs	Domestic Dogs
Where They Live		
Diet		
Type of Dwelling		
Sounds Made		
Animal Family		

Directions: Write answers to the questions. Be sure to use complete sentences.

1. What are three main differences between prairie dogs and domestic dogs?

_____

_____

_____

2. How do you think the lives of prairie dogs differ from wild members of the dog family, such as wolves?

_____

_____

_____

3. What conclusions can you draw about prairie dogs because of the way in which their towns are built?

_____

_____

_____

Amber

Where can you find 100 million-year-old dinosaur blood? From amber, a substance known more for its decorative uses than for its scientific value—that is, until recently.

Amber is actually hardened tree resin that has been fossilized. Most of it is mined in the Baltic Sea area. It is smooth and warms quickly to the touch. Amber has been valued as a gemstone since prehistoric times. The ancient Greeks called it "electron," perhaps because amber builds up a small, negative charge when it is rubbed. The Romans thought that amber had medicinal properties. It also was used as a type of currency in ancient trade routes. Most often, amber is translucent red, yellow, orange, or gold—colors that were rare and valued. It was used for jewelry and for good-luck charms.

Perhaps the height of amber's decorative powers could be seen in a Russian palace. In the 1700s, an entire room of 100,000 carved and interlocking amber pieces was given as a gift to Tsar Peter the Great. This golden room, lit by more than 500 candles, was said to be dazzling in its beauty. However, the room is now missing. The Nazis stole the room during World War II, dismantling and hiding it. A replica is being made of the room from drawings and paintings, but the search continues for the original, which is now worth approximately $200 million.

Today, the focus on amber has changed from decorative to scientific. This gemstone helps scientists learn about life millions of years ago. One in every 100 pieces of amber currently mined in the Dominican Republic contains a plant, insect, or tiny animal from prehistoric times. The once-living matter fossilized in amber can tell us about animal and plant diversity, the ecology of the landscape, and even how living things interacted with each other. Because of discoveries captured in amber, scientists have had to revise some of their evolutionary theories.

An even bigger breakthrough has been the ability to isolate and identify DNA of insects found in amber. This ability may one day lead to the isolation of dinosaur DNA. How? If a fossilized insect bit a dinosaur, it may be carrying that DNA. The problem is being able to recognize dinosaur DNA from millions of other sequences.

From art to science, the amazing story of amber continues!

Amber (cont.)

Directions: Write **F** for fact or **O** for opinion for each sentence.

1._____ Amber is hardened tree resin that has been fossilized.

2._____ Because of amber, scientists have had to revise some theories about evolution.

3._____ DNA research is the most significant scientific breakthrough this planet has ever known.

4._____ Most amber is mined in the Baltic Sea area.

5._____ The amber room was the most beautiful work of architecture in the 1700s.

6._____ The amber room of Tsar Peter the Great is being recreated, but the original is missing.

7._____ The amber room of Tsar Peter the Great is worth approximately $200 million.

8. _____ Many pieces of amber contain fossilized insects, plants, or animals.

9. _____ The study of dinosaur DNA is very dangerous.

10._____ Amber could probably be used as medicine again, just as the Romans used it.

Directions: Write an answer to the question.

11. In your opinion, what is the most important role that amber has to play in our civilization? Explain your opinion.

_____

_____

_____

_____

A Letter to Camilla

November 25, 1963

Dear Camilla,

Today was the saddest day in American history. I wish you could have seen my whole family watching the funeral on TV in absolute silence. Mrs. Kennedy wore a black veil over her hair. She seemed very brave to me. She held the hands of her two children, John and Caroline. The casket was pulled to the church on a caisson, which is usually used to pull a cannon. It seemed fitting to me that this, like so many details of the funeral, were taken from Abraham Lincoln's funeral ceremony. I can't imagine that people then could possibly feel as shocked as we do today.

I don't think I will ever forget the muffled drums, the trumpet playing taps, or the riderless horse, which symbolized a fallen leader. I think that was a more powerful symbol than the missing jet fighter from the V-formation that flew overhead. What will this country do without our great leader? I kept thinking about that as the day wore on.

My mother and aunts cried all during the funeral. My father said the funeral made him feel old and tired. Tonight, I feel tired, too...and sad, and scared. I think that every person in the United States is scared tonight. How could this terrible thing have happened?

Your pen pal,
Jessica

A Letter to Camilla (cont.)

Directions: Write **F** for fact or **O** for opinion for each sentence.

1. _____ "A Letter to Camilla" is about the funeral of President John F. Kennedy.

2. _____ The funeral of John F. Kennedy was the saddest day in American history.

3. _____ John F. Kennedy's funeral was based on the funeral of Abraham Lincoln.

4. _____ It was fitting that Kennedy's funeral be based on the death of another great leader.

5. _____ The riderless horse was the most powerful symbol of a fallen leader at the funeral.

6. _____ Another symbol of a fallen leader was a missing fighter jet from an overhead formation.

7. _____ The people of 1963 were more shocked by a presidential assassination than people of the Civil War era.

8. _____ On the evening of November 25, 1963, everyone in America felt sad and tired.

9. _____ Mrs. Kennedy had two children.

Directions: Write a response to the question. Be sure to give a reason for your opinion.

10. In your opinion, which was the greater loss: the death of Abraham Lincoln or the death of John F. Kennedy?

_____

_____

_____

_____

_____

Tramp Art

A man stood outside a general store on a day in the mid-1930s. He unwrapped the tattered flour sack from around a wooden object. Holding up the object for inspection by the first store patron who appeared, he asked, "Could you use a picture frame?"

The frame was an example of tramp art. The man had fashioned the frame from thin layers of wood. Tiny V-shaped notches decorated the edges of each quarter-inch layer. He cut each layer narrower than the one beneath it, and then stacked them. Glue held the layers together, and a dab of yellow paint dotted each notch. The notches and thin layers created an intricate, geometrical design.

This folk-art form probably began in Europe, where fathers taught their sons the craft. In America, most tramp art was created during the Depression. Desperate men known as tramps left their homes and roamed the country, vainly looking for work. Rather than accept handouts of food to survive, some chose to make objects to sell. Poverty forced the artists to scavenge wood and glue for their projects. Cigar boxes and fruit crates often furnished the wood. Many tramp artists created picture frames, but some also built bigger objects such as desks and chests. Some artists smoothed and burnished their wooden pieces to a deep luster, and others also painted them when they could scavenge small amounts of paint.

Today, folk art is increasingly popular and tramp art from the 1930s has become valuable in the antiques market. A group of formerly homeless men recently formed an artists' group to make and sell new tramp art. By working together, these men have been luckier than tramps of the Depression. They have built a thriving business and have been able to buy homes for themselves. When you see a piece of tramp art, old or new, remember that this art grew out of a struggle for survival and the desire to express oneself through art.

Tramp Art (cont.)

Directions: Read each sentence. Then write a new sentence that turns the opinion into a fact.

1. During the Depression, the worst economic crisis the world has ever known, many people were unable to find jobs.

    _____
    _____
    _____

2. Tramps traveled to look for work, but probably would have been better off staying in one place.

    _____
    _____
    _____

3. Tramp art, a folk art from Europe, is one of the most beautiful crafts of the 20th century.

    _____
    _____
    _____

4. The best tramp art has intricate, geometrical designs.

    _____
    _____
    _____

5. Tramps scavanged materials so that their art would look better than other peoples.

    _____
    _____
    _____

6. It's strange that this art is considered valuable today.

    _____
    _____
    _____

Northern Lights

For thousands of years, people have seen the northern lights, <u>multicolored rays of light</u> streaking upward in the sky. Many Native American tribes thought that the lights were an omen, <u>a sign of something to come</u>. Some tribes thought that the lights were an omen of war. Others believed that they were human spirits carrying torches to the sky. The Inuit people believed that the lights were the <u>spirits of seals, caribou, and whales</u>.

Europeans had different reactions to the northern lights. In 37 A.D., a group of people living outside of Ostia, Italy, thought that the colony of Ostia was on fire. Rushing to the rescue, they found no fire except the fiery lights in the sky. In 1583, people in France who saw the lights flocked to churches to pray. <u>They superstitiously believed</u> that the lights were an omen of the end of the world.

The northern lights have a scientific name: *aurora borealis*. <u>They are solar-powered</u>. The sun emits charged particles in all directions. A cloud of these particles is called <u>plasma</u>. The stream of plasma coming from the sun is called the solar wind. When the solar wind disturbs the Earth's magnetic field, the particles glow and create the aurora borealis.

These lights, although beautiful, can create a lot of problems because of the great amount of energy they use. <u>One display</u> can use as much energy as is used by the entire population of the United States in a day! The charged particles bounce around the planet's magnetic field and cause atmospheric disturbance that affects a number of objects. Compasses point the wrong way, communications systems <u>can be disrupted</u>, and power systems can go out. Satellite computers can malfunction. Once, taxi drivers in Alaska received radio dispatches from a cab company in New Jersey! You can imagine the confusion that caused.

The aurora borealis sometimes lights up the sky with bands of pink, red, green, and blue rays of light. At other times, they are colorless but look like long curtains waving across the sky. Newscasters and weather people usually report when the northern lights are performing. Try to catch <u>this information</u> so you won't miss <u>the show</u>.

Northern Lights (cont.)

Directions: Look at the underlined words or phrases in the story. Then decide to what or whom each phrase or word refers.

1. To what does <u>multicolored rays of light</u> refer?

   _____

2. To what does <u>a sign of something to come</u> refer?

   _____

3. To what does <u>spirits of seals, caribou, and whales</u> refer?

   _____

4. To what does <u>They superstitiously believed</u> refer?

   _____

5. To what does <u>They are solar-powered</u> refer?

   _____

6. To what does <u>plasma</u> refer?

   _____

7. To what does <u>One display</u> refer?

   _____

8. To what does <u>can be disrupted</u> refer?

   _____

9. To what does <u>this information</u> refer?

   _____

10. To what does <u>the show</u> refer?

   _____

Directions: Write a response to the following.

11. Imagine you are the leader of a northern tribe. Write a short tale to tell your tribe what the lights are and what they mean.

   _____

   _____

   _____

   _____

   _____

   _____

   _____

Remarkable Rooms

You may find more comfortable surroundings, but it would be hard to find more unique overnight stays than in these four loony lodgings.

The first hotel on our tour is Jules's Undersea Lodge, named after Jules Verne who wrote *Twenty Thousand Leagues Under the Sea*. This two-room lodge is anchored to the floor of a lagoon in Key Largo, Florida. <u>Once an underwater mobile research lab</u>, it was converted into a hotel in 1986. Because its entrance can only be reached by scuba diving, guests can pack only the necessities in one small, waterproof suitcase. Televisions in the rooms play only water-themed videos, such as *The Little Mermaid* or *Splash*. The hotel actually has room service and its own chef. If you order a pizza for dinner, a hotel employee will dive down to your room with <u>a large pepperoni-and-cheese</u> in a watertight container.

If an underwater adventure doesn't appeal to you, let's move on to the Ariau Jungle Hotel in Brazil. All of the 138 rooms in <u>this spacious hotel</u> are built on stilts and touch the treetops of the Amazon rainforest. One room sits atop a tree on the banks of the Rio Negro. It <u>can be reached only by boat</u>. Guests can swim in a pool, play in a game room, or go on searches for alligators and piranhas. In your room, monkeys swinging past your windows will entertain you. Be sure not to feed <u>these treetop acrobats</u> or your room will be overrun with them!

For the budget-minded, a Japanese capsule hotel is the place to go. These rooms <u>resemble microwaves</u> from the outside; a small door swings outward. The inside is only several feet wide and about six feet (1.8 m) long. You crawl into your room at night, right onto your bed, which takes up the entire floor. You can sit, but not stand. Providing inexpensive nights

of sleep for commuters who miss their train home to the suburbs, these hotels are also used for business travel. Each capsule has a television and a radio. There's no room service, but you can buy food from vending machines in the lobby.

The Ice Hotel in Jukkasjarvi, Sweden, is our last stop. It's made entirely of ice and snow. The rooms are not heated. Even the beds are made from snow, <u>frozen into solid rectangles</u>. For warmth, each guest is given reindeer skins and a sleeping bag. <u>This frozen accommodation</u> melts each spring and then is reconstructed every fall. Guests go dog-sledding or join snowmobile safaris. The hotel's dining room features salmon soup and roast reindeer. You should plan on bringing a coat, gloves, and a hat to <u>this icy restaurant!</u>

Remarkable Rooms (cont.)

Directions: Look at the underlined words or phrases in the story. Then decide to what or whom each phrase or word refers.

1. To what does <u>an underwater mobile research lab</u> refer?

   _____

2. To what does a <u>large pepperoni-and-cheese</u> refer?

   _____

3. To what does <u>this spacious hotel</u> refer?

   _____

4. To what does <u>It can be reached only by boat</u> refer?

   _____

5. To what does <u>these treetop acrobats</u> refer?

   _____

6. To what does <u>resemble microwaves</u> refer?

   _____

7. To what does <u>frozen into solid rectangles</u> refer?

   _____

8. To what does <u>This frozen accommodation</u> refer?

   _____

9. To what does <u>this icy restaurant</u> refer?

   _____

Directions: Write a response to the question.

10. At which one of the four hotels in the story would you choose to stay? Be sure to describe the reason for your choice.

   _____

   _____

   _____

   _____

   _____

   _____

   _____

Walls of Water

After a quiet night of fishing in 1896, the Japanese fishing crew set sail for their village. As the shoreline came into view, they were stunned by what they saw. The village lay in a heap. It looked like a giant had come and pounded the houses flat, then tossed them in all directions.

In a sense, a giant had paid a visit. A giant wave called a *tsunami* caused the devastation. It killed roughly 22,000 people up and down the coastline of Japan on that night in June more than a century ago. But this was far from an isolated incident. Tsunamis have stormed like angry monsters in many places around the globe, from New Guinea to the United States. What causes these great sea waves?

A tsunami can occur after an earthquake, an underwater landslide, or a volcanic eruption. Large volumes of water are displaced and form into columns of water. The name, *tsunami*, means "harbor wave." At sea, the waves are not usually a problem. But when a tsunami reaches shallow water, like a harbor, it can build to an enormous height before crashing into the shore. Some of these waves look like four-story buildings. They are also fast; a tsunami can travel as fast as a jet airplane.

People have little warning when tsunamis hit. In the Pacific Rim countries, the population knows to be cautious after an earthquake or volcanic activity. But an underwater landslide is hidden, like a secret, until the tsunami that it causes moves toward shore. Underwater shelves, like terraces in a field, form where rivers empty into an ocean. Seismic activity can cause the shelf to crumble. The loose sediment cascades down like an avalanche. A tsunami can result from the displaced water.

Japan is the unlucky recipient of the most tsunamis. Next are Chile and Hawaii. United

States citizens often have felt the power of these gigantic waves. In 1958, a couple named Bill and Vivian Swanson were fishing on a trawler in an Alaskan bay. At ten o'clock, they felt the boat deck shake and saw a rock avalanche shower down from a nearby mountain. The rocks roared into the bay like a herd of buffalo. The resulting wave was taller than the Sears Tower in Chicago and moved toward their boat at a speed of 100 miles an hour. It flung the trawler to its crest, snapping its anchor line. Miraculously, air formed like a bubble inside the bow of the boat, giving the Swansons just enough time to escape.

In the past 100 years, more than 50,000 people have lost their lives to these disastrous waves. Because tsunamis are not everyday events, people tend to forget their power. Scientists, however, are working to develop new ways of detecting tsunamis so that better warning systems can be created.

Walls of Water (cont.)

Directions: Write **S** next to the sentences that contain similes. Write **X** next to the sentences that do not contain similes.

1. _____ The village lay in a heap.

2. _____ It looked like a giant had come and pounded the houses flat.

3. _____ Tsunamis have stormed like angry monsters in many places around the globe.

4. _____ Large volumes of water are displaced and form into columns of water.

5. _____ When a tsunami reaches shallow water, like a harbor, it can build to an enormous height.

6. _____ Some of these waves look like four-story buildings.

7. _____ An underwater landslide is hidden, like a secret.

8. _____ The loose sediment cascades down like an avalanche.

9. _____ They felt the deck shake and saw a rock avalanche shower down from a mountain.

10. _____ The rocks roared into the bay like a herd of buffalo.

11. Write a three-sentence summary of the reading selection *Walls of Water*. Include at least one simile in your summary.

_____

_____

_____

_____

_____

The Birthday

The house was a cloud of secrets. My family had whispering conversations, which sounded like paper rustling. My heart would flutter like a bird. I knew they were talking about my birthday and surprises.

Packages arrived in the mail from relatives. The gifts were bright flowers, wrapped in shining paper and set aside for the big day. I knew that a party was being planned, but I did not know any details.

My mother started baking. She made a cake that looked like a big, pink drum. She baked cookies that were snowdrifts of powdered sugar. She baked bread for the sandwiches. The house smelled like a bakery.

My birthday was a ship, sailing closer and closer to shore.

Directions: Write **S** if the sentence contains a simile. Write **M** if the sentence contains a metaphor.

1. _____ The house was a cloud of secrets.

2. _____ My family had whispering conversations, which sounded like paper rustling.

3. _____ My heart would flutter like a bird.

4. _____ The gifts were bright flowers, wrapped in shining paper.

5. _____ She made a cake that looked like a big, pink drum.

6. _____ She baked cookies that were snowdrifts of powdered sugar.

7. _____ The house smelled like a bakery.

8. _____ My birthday was a ship, sailing closer and closer to shore.

The Birthday (cont.)

Directions: Match two parts of each sentence to create metaphors about a birthday.

9. The cake   were boxes of delight.

10. The gifts   were bursts of noise
    and excitement.

11. The games   was a sweet dream of chocolate.

Directions: Match two parts of each sentence to create similes about a birthday.

12. The guests   was like a detective, tracking down cake crumbs.

13. The dog   were like a community of friends.

14. The house   was like a bright flower with its colorful decorations.

Directions: Write each simile as a metaphor.

15. Her skin was like peaches and cream.

_____

_____

16. His smile was like a beacon of light.

_____

_____

17. The cat was like a jungle animal as it stalked the mouse.

_____

_____

Rhyme Schemes

Poetry discusses feelings, ideas, or events. Sometimes a poem recounts a tale from history or legend. Other times, a poem presents a simple image that symbolizes an emotion or captures one moment in time. Some poems do not rhyme, but some do. Poems that do rhyme have identifiable *rhyme schemes*. The rhyme scheme is identified by using alphabet letters to identify the pairs of lines that rhyme. Sometimes these rhyming lines are together, and sometimes they are separated.

Here is an example:

a A timeless tree stood
b on the edge of a dream.
a And thought that it could
b run like the stream.

Because *stood* and *could* rhyme, the lines that end in those words are marked with an **a**. *Dream* and *stream* rhyme, so the lines that end in those words are marked with a **b**.

Directions: Match the missing words to each stanza to complete the rhyme schemes.

1. _____ City noises, crowded street;
   Country sun, rows of _____.

   A. tell

2. _____ In an alley, a flower grows.
   It stands alone, an upturned bell.
   How did it get there? The wind knows,
   A secret it will never _____.

   B. shore

3. _____ A shower of tears rains down on the _____.
   This mountain and I are both soaked to the bone.

   C. end

4. _____ As she walked along the _____,
   She found some shells but wanted more.

   D. stone

5. _____ My loyal dog, a noble friend,
   Has sadly met his mortal _____.

   E. wheat

Ballad of a Cherry Pie

We met by yonder cherry tree.
I glanced at her, she winked at me.
I offered her a slice of pie.
How could I know our love would die?

After a bite, her watery eyes
Gazed at me; she gave a cry
And gagged; she turned and ran away.
I have not seen her since that day.

You see, I like my pie with spice.
Chili powder tastes so nice!
But my love I lost, so now I cry...
Say, would you like a piece of pie?

by Norm Sneller

Directions: Circle the correct answer.

1. What makes this poem a ballad?

    A. the rhyme scheme

    B. the fact that it tells a story

    C. the rhythm of the poem

    D. the imagery

2. What is the poet's intent in this ballad?

    A. to tell a tragic tale

    B. to question the nature of love

    C. to present the story of a historical event

    D. to create a humorous version of the ballad form

3. Why did the speaker lose his love?

    A. because the woman ran away

    B. because he gave her pie with chili powder in it

    C. because he gave up love for baking

    D. because he lost his love's address

4. What elements of this ballad match more traditional ballads?

    A. it tells a story of lost love

    B. it tells a story about a baker

    C. it captures a battle in a war

    D. it tells of a love triangle between three people

5. Write a one-sentence summary of this ballad.

    _____

    _____

The Bee Is Not Afraid of Me

The bee is not afraid of me,
I know the butterfly.
The pretty people in the woods
Receive me cordially.

The brooks laugh louder when I come,
The breezes madder play.
Wherefore, mine eyes, thy silver mists?
Wherefore, O summer's day?

by Emily Dickinson

Directions: Circle the correct answer.

1. What makes this poem a lyric?

   A. It tells the story of a historical event.

   B. It is short, musical, and reveals the emotion of the speaker.

   C. It is written in a special pattern of syllables.

   D. It expresses sadness over someone who has died.

2. What is the purpose of this lyric poem?

   A. to express the poet's feelings about nature

   B. to show the habits of bees and butterflies

   C. to speak to the nature of death

   D. to reflect on a lost love

3. What are "the pretty people in the woods"?

   A. neighbors who live in a house in the woods

   B. tramps who are camping in the woods

   C. fairies and elves

   D. birds, animals, and insects

4. What traditional elements of a lyric are found in this poem?

   A. It is written in first person and expresses the emotions of the poet.

   B. It is written in third person and expresses the thoughts of the poet.

   C. It is written in third person and describes a series of actions.

   D. It is written in first person and tells of a true historical event.

5. Write a one-sentence summary of this poem.

   _____

   _____

   _____

Three Haiku by Bashō

(1) At the ancient pond
a green frog plunges into
the sound of water.

(2) Come outdoors to view
the truth of flowers blooming
amid poverty.

(3) Sick on my journey,
only my dreams will wander
these desolate moors.

Directions: Circle the correct answer.

1. What makes these three poems haiku?

   A. They are stories of journeys made by Japanese poets.

   B. They have a specific syllable pattern and offer insights through aspects of nature.

   C. They are lyrical poems about tragedy and loss.

   D. They have topics based on true historical events.

2. What is the pattern of haiku?

   A. first line: seven syllables; second line: five syllables; third line: five syllables

   B. first line: five syllables; second line: five syllables; third line: seven syllables

   C. first line: five syllables; second line: seven syllables; third line: five syllables

   D. first line: seven syllables; second line: seven syllables; third line: five syllables

3. What is the theme of haiku number 2?

   A. Frogs dive into the sound of water, not water itself.

   B. Even in poverty, people can take comfort in the beauty of nature.

   C. Flowers are truthful and honest.

   D. The moors are sad and lonely.

4. What happens in haiku number 3?

   A. The poet is ill and cannot hike across the moors.

   B. The poet sees flowers and takes heart in their beauty.

   C. The poet hikes across the moors and then becomes ill.

   D. The poet dreams that he becomes ill on a journey.

5. Write a haiku about your favorite season.

_____

_____

_____

Ode to Autumn

Season of mists and mellow fruitfulness!
Close bosom-friend of the maturing sun;
Conspiring with him how to load and bless
With fruit the vines that round the thatch-eaves run;
To bend with apples the moss'd cottage-trees,
And fill all fruit with ripeness to the core;
To swell the gourd, and plump the hazel shells
With a sweet kernel; to set budding more,
And still more, later flowers for the bees,
Until they think warm days will never cease,
For Summer has o'er-brimmed their clammy cells.
           by John Keats

Directions: Circle the correct answer.

1. What makes this poem an ode?

   A. It shows grief for something lost or dead.

   B. It is a formal poem of praise for someone or something.

   C. It tells the story of an actual historical event.

   D. It has fourteen lines written in iambic pentameter.

2. The excerpt above is only one stanza of the ode. The other stanzas probably contain—

   A. praise for autumn's plentiful harvest and weather.

   B. a description of a death that took place during the fall of the year.

   C. three lines each with five, seven, and five syllables.

   D. complaints about autumn rain and frost.

3. To what does the poet refer in the phrase "their clammy cells"?

   A. the petals of a flower

   B. the honey cells of a beehive

   C. the prison cells in the local jail

   D. the biological cells in a hazelnut

4. List five things that you would praise about your favorite season.

   A. _____

   _____

   B. _____

   _____

   C. _____

   _____

   D. _____

   _____

◆◆◆◆◆◆◆◆◆◆◆◆◆◆◆◆◆◆◆◆◆◆◆◆◆◆◆◆◆◆◆◆◆◆

Pebble Rings, Like Memories

The old stone bridge across Rügen Bay
Is one of my favorite places to play.
I toss pebbles for Mom, and a pebble for Dad,
And a rock for the horses and chickens we had.
I watch as each of the stones makes rings
Like the song that each of my memories sings.
For my wife—for my dear and precious Lenore—
My hands and my eyes throw several more.
And then, before my playing is done
I throw the most important one,
For the memory of my son.

　　　　　　　by Robert Hatfield

Directions: Write an answer to each question about the poem.

1. What makes this poem an elegy?

    _____

2. Write one example of a simile from the poem.

    _____

3. Write two pairs of rhyming words from the poem.

    _____

4. How old does the speaker seem at the end of the poem?

    _____

5. Is the speaker happy or sad? How do you know?

    _____

The Eagle

He clasps the crag with crooked hands;
Close to the sea in lonely lands,
Ring'd with the azure world, he stands.

The wrinkled sea beneath him crawls;
He watches from his mountain walls,
And like a thunderbolt, he falls.
            by Alfred, Lord Tennyson

Directions: Write an answer to each question.

1. Write a short summary of this poem. What is the poem about?

    _____

    _____

2. What simile appears in this poem?

    _____

3. What does the poet mean by "the azure world"?

    _____

4. Would you classify this poem as a ballad, an elegy, or a lyric poem? Give a reason for your choice.

    _____

    _____

5. What is the rhyme scheme of this poem?

    _____

Name _____ Date _____

We Crouch in Caves

We crouch in caves of dirt and coal,
Our bodies stiff and fingers wrapped with tape.
This place is an endless ebony tunnel.
With counted beats, our muscles strong and tight
Chip away at walls of rock.
Faster now to fight the clock,
The air resounds with the sound of picks;
With steady rhythm in our souls,
We work in pairs, my dad and I.
We dream secret dreams
Until the whistle leaves us spent but done.
by Elaine Dion

Directions: Write an answer to each question.

1. Write a short summary of this poem. What is the poem about?

    _____

    _____

2. What metaphor appears in this poem?

    _____

3. What does the poet mean by "we dream secret dreams"?

    _____

    _____

4. Who are the two people described in the poem?

    _____

    _____

5. How would you describe the tone of this poem?

    _____

Ozymandias

I met a traveller from an antique land
Who said: Two vast and trunkless legs of stone
Stand in the desert...Near them, on the sand,
Half sunk, a shattered visage lies, whose frown,
And wrinkled lip, and sneer of cold command,
Tell that its sculptor well those passions read
Which yet survive, stamped on these lifeless things,
The hand that mocked them, and the heart that fed:
And on the pedestal these words appear:
"My name is Ozymandias, king of kings:
Look on my works, ye Mighty, and despair!"
Nothing beside remains. Round the decay
Of that colossal wreck, boundless and bare
The lone and level sands stretch far away.
                    by Percy Bysshe Shelley

Directions: Circle the correct answer.

1. Choose the best description of *irony*.

    A. conveying something different or even opposite from the literal meaning

    B. characterized by a hard, cold attitude

    C. easily annoyed or distracted

    D. conveying something firm and inflexible

2. What is the irony in the poem "Ozymandias"?

    A. The sculpture of the great king had fallen apart.

    B. The person telling the story was awed by the great works of Ozymandias.

    C. The pedestal inscription indicates a great kingdom, but there is nothing left but desert.

    D. The legs of stone belonged to a king who was killed by his subjects.

3. What is the best description of the statue?

    A. Two legs are still standing. The head of the sculpture is half buried in the sand.

    B. The head of the sculpture is on the pedestal, and two legs are lying nearby.

    C. The head of the sculpture and a stone heart are lying a pedestal.

    D. The body of the statue is still whole, but the legs are missing.

4. What is the best description of the face of the statue?

    A. The expression is warm and welcoming.

    B. The expression is blank and conveys nothing.

    C. The expression is cold and sneering.

    D. The expression is serious and confident.

Food for Thought

The waiter was taking a break outside the back door of the restaurant. He said to a brand-new employee, "You just have to be the one <u>to break the ice</u> with the chef. Sometimes it seems like he has <u>a chip on his shoulder</u>, but he's okay. But this is a busy place. You've <u>jumped out of the frying pan and into the fire</u>, let me tell you. I hope you don't have any <u>pie-in-the-sky</u> ideas about taking things easy here. Some days, I feel like I'm <u>going bananas</u>. It might not be <u>your cup of tea</u>. I think we've got <u>the cream of the crop</u> here; everybody does a great job. It's hard sometimes not to <u>fly off the handle</u> when things are so hectic, though. <u>In a nutshell</u>, I think you'll do all right if you don't mind hard work."

Directions: Match each idiom with its meaning.

1. _____ to break the ice

2. _____ a chip on his shoulder

3. _____ out of the frying pan and into the fire

4. _____ pie-in-the-sky

5. _____ going bananas

6. _____ your cup of tea

7. _____ the cream of the crop

8. _____ fly off the handle

9. _____ in a nutshell

A. unrealistic

B. something one enjoys

C. the best available

D. to make a start

E. to lose one's temper

F. seemingly angry or resentful

G. go crazy

H. from a bad situation to worse one

I. to sum up

The Good Bacteria

What do you get if you mix <u>common</u> bacteria and vinegar? This is not the beginning of a joke. It is a serious scientific question. The answer is, you get bacteria that eat toxic <u>waste</u> and turn that waste into salt.

Bacteria can make you sick, but not all <u>strains</u> of bacteria are harmful. Some bacteria benefit human beings. Scientists have proposed a new, <u>beneficial</u> use for bacteria called bioremediation. Bioremediation uses specialized microorganisms for <u>toxic</u> cleanup. Vinegar stimulates these bacteria to consume the toxic liquids. The bacteria transform the toxins into salt. The bacteria <u>function</u> in closed-in places, without sunlight, and they produce oxygen as a by-product. Some scientists are even exploring whether these bacteria could be put to use in mines or during <u>prolonged</u> space travel, where they could digest waste products and produce additional oxygen.

Other scientists wonder whether bacteria could be used to digest radioactive wastes. Scientists <u>introduced</u> one type of bacteria into water that contained dissolved uranium. The bacteria went to work, transforming the uranium-laden water into water mixed with a harmless solid. Geneticists—scientists who study genes—propose <u>customizing</u> bacteria to work on specific types of wastes, including nuclear wastes. Experiments have included inserting genes from one bacteria into another type of bacteria, creating a "superbug." Laboratory tests show that the superbug transforms toxic mercury in nuclear waste into less toxic forms of the substance.

The Good Bacteria (cont.)

Directions: Look at the underlined words in the story. Then circle the correct answer.

1. As used in the article, <u>common</u> means—
   A. multiple.
   B. ordinary.
   C. lower-class.
   D. poisonous.

2. As used in the article, <u>waste</u> means—
   A. misuse.
   B. litter.
   C. unwanted by-products.
   D. leftovers.

3. As used in the article, <u>strains</u> means—
   A. types.
   B. injuries.
   C. twists.
   D. pulls.

4. As used in the article, <u>beneficial</u> means—
   A. cutting-edge.
   B. ordinary.
   C. advantageous.
   D. extraordinary.

5. As used in the article, <u>toxic</u> means—
   A. playful.
   B. unscientific.
   C. uncorrupted.
   D. poisonous.

6. As used in the article, <u>function</u> means—
   A. multiply.
   B. divide.
   C. work.
   D. care.

7. As used in the article, <u>prolonged</u> means—
   A. extended.
   B. introductory.
   C. optimistic.
   D. enduring.

8. As used in the article, <u>introduced</u> means—
   A. begun.
   B. exchange names.
   C. added.
   D. started.

9. As used in the article, <u>customizing</u> means—
   A. mannered.
   B. tailoring.
   C. injecting.
   D. poisoning.

10. Write a new sentence that contains the word "geneticist."

_____

_____

Leonardo's Way of Seeing

Leonardo da Vinci believed in *saper vedere*, or the power of observation. While his contemporaries looked for scientific truth in the writings of ancient scholars, da Vinci's theories were based on empirical research, that which he observed and recorded in his many notebooks.

"How does the human body work?" da Vinci asked himself. To answer this question, da Vinci learned to dissect cadavers—usually the bodies of dead criminals. He then made thousands of detailed sketches of their muscles, organs, and skeletons.

LEONARDO DAVINCI

Directions: Choose **true** or **false** to answer each question.

1. *Saper vedere* and *the power of observation* most likely mean the same thing.

    A. true

    B. false

2. Empirical research is based on observations.

    A. true

    B. false

3. When da Vinci *recorded* his observations, it means he made audio versions of them.

    A. true

    B. false

4. The word *cadaver* and the word *criminal* mean the same thing.

    A. true

    B. alse

5. Leonardo da Vinci probably made sketches of the heart.

    A. true

    B. false

6. In the context of the passage above, *empirical* means "minor."

    A. true

    B. false

7. Leonardo da Vinci conducted his research exactly like other Renaissance scientists.

    A. true

    B. false

8. To *dissect* something means "to cut it apart."

    A. true

    B. false

Analogies

An *analogy* finds the similarities between two things that are primarily dissimilar. To do that, the analogy makes a comparison. If you were to say, "A meteor is to an astronomer as a geode is to a geologist," you would be making an analogy. You are saying that one object (the meteor) is studied by one type of scientist in a similar way that another object (the geode) is studied by a different kind of scientist. In this way, you are showing a connection between them.

Directions: Circle the correct answer to complete each analogy.

1. Lava is to volcano as stalactite is to _____.

   A. moon

   B. ocean

   C. island

   D. cave

2. Moldy is to rancid as edict is to _____.

   A. eviction

   B. proclamation

   C. conviction

   D. cheese

3. World Wide Web is to www as self-contained underwater breathing apparatus is to _____.

   A. SCUBA

   B. NASA

   C. HTML

   D. SUV

4. Stomach is to digestion as lung is to _____.

   A. transpiration

   B. respiration

   C. dehydration

   D. circulation

5. Author is to essay as composer is to _____.

   A. orchestra

   B. fortissimo

   C. symphonic

   D. concerto

6. Milliliter is to liter as meter is to _____.

   A. kilometer

   B. centimeter

   C. millimeter

   D. decimeter

7. Quadruped is to cat as biped is to _____.

   A. human

   B. millipede

   C. dog

   D. fish

8. Paris is to France as Rome is to _____.

   A. England

   B. Greece

   C. Florence

   D. Italy

Survival

What would you do if you were <u>stranded</u> in the wilderness? You have probably read or heard about people who survive under seemingly impossible conditions. These people have been able to survive by focusing on three basic needs: water, food, and shelter.

Water is one of the few substances necessary to <u>sustain</u> life, but pure water may be difficult to find. Water can be <u>purified</u> by boiling it for three to five minutes. If there is a shortage of water, do not overexert yourself. Overexertion will cause you to <u>perspire</u> excessively, resulting in a salt deficiency that causes cramps, fatigue, and dehydration.

Feelings of hunger can be ignored with a positive attitude, but food is another necessity if you are lost or stranded for a longer period of time. Some people have to overcome their <u>aversion</u> to eating insects, earthworms, grasshoppers, and other animals that are easy to catch. Plants, however, should not be eaten unless they are identified as <u>edible</u>. Nuts are easy to identify and are nutritious. Knobby berries, such as blackberries and raspberries, are also simple to identify. You can also eat inner tree bark and the shoots of pine saplings. Pine needles can be simmered in hot water to produce a tea.

Protection from extreme temperatures is another concern. In heavy rains or snow, you can crawl under the snow or <u>vegetation</u> for shelter. A <u>makeshift</u> cave can be created by

tunneling into the base of a thick evergreen tree, and using the tree <u>boughs</u> to line and insulate the cave. Clothing or other fabric can be used if you need to shield yourself from hot sun.

Remaining calm is extremely important in any emergency. Come up with a plan and don't waste time or energy by getting upset. Find a water source, identify food to gather, and find shelter. By focusing on these basics, you can turn yourself into a survivor.

Survival (cont.)

Directions: Look at the underlined words in the story. Then circle the correct answer.

1. As used in the article, <u>stranded</u> means—
   A. separated.
   B. upright.
   C. marooned.
   D. found.

2. As used in the article, <u>sustain</u> means—
   A. extend.
   B. maintain.
   C. direct.
   D. hold.

3. As used in the article, <u>purified</u> means—
   A. cleansed.
   B. baked.
   C. twisted.
   D. destroyed.

4. As used in the article, <u>perspire</u> means—
   A. think.
   B. sweat.
   C. lunge.
   D. dehydrate.

5. As used in the article, <u>aversion</u> means—
   A. attraction.
   B. repugnance.
   C. corrupted.
   D. poisonous.

6. As used in the article, <u>edible</u> means—
   A. fit to be eaten.
   B. easy to cook.
   C. corrected.
   D. harvested.

7. As used in the article, <u>vegetation</u> means—
   A. animal life.
   B. roots.
   C. plant life.
   D. lazy.

8. As used in the article, <u>makeshift</u> means—
   A. sturdy.
   B. timely.
   C. portable.
   D. temporary.

9. As used in the article, <u>boughs</u> means—
   A. needles.
   B. branches.
   C. leaves.
   D. trunks.

10. Write a new sentence that contains the word "overexertion." Use the information from the article to help you.

    _____
    _____
    _____
    _____
    _____

Time for Lunch

◆ ◆ ◆ ◆ ◆ MENU ◆ ◆ ◆ ◆ ◆

Hamburger with a <u>handful</u> of potato chips	$4.00
Hamburger with <u>scores</u> of potato chips	$6.00
Sandwich of thinly <u>carved</u> turkey	$5.00
Hot dog with very <u>hot</u> relish	$3.50
Fresh shrimp—you <u>discard</u> the shells!	$7.50
An <u>entrée</u> of fish with mixed-greens salad	$8.00
Spaghetti cooked in a large <u>kettle</u>	$4.50
Salad with crunchy <u>croutons</u> on top	$3.50
Apple pie from a farm-fresh <u>crop</u> of apples	$2.50

Directions: Look at the underlined words in the menu.
Then circle each word's meaning as it is used in the menu.

1. handful
   A. measured by hand
   B. a small amount
   C. a large amount
   D. crushed

2. scores
   A. sheets of music
   B. a small amount
   C. a large amount
   D. ratings

3. carved
   A. cut
   B. chopped
   C. corner
   D. drawn

4. hot
   A. warm
   B. spicy
   C. burned
   D. dressed

5. discard
   A. keep
   B. merge
   C. create
   D. toss aside

6. entrée
   A. entrance
   B. main dish
   C. snack
   D. exit

7. kettle
   A. drum
   B. drawer
   C. frying pan
   D. large pot

8. croutons
   A. bread crumbs
   B. bread slices
   C. dried bread cubes
   D. toast with butter

9. crop
   A. produce supply
   B. riding equipment
   C. new plants
   D. fruit

62

Recipe for Success

Aunt Millie's Party Cake

To bake this cake, you need to <u>acquire</u> one fresh egg. Next, add just a <u>dab</u> of butter. It is absolutely <u>critical</u> to use exactly 237 ml of sugar. Choose a mixing <u>gadget</u> and mix thoroughly. Add <u>sufficient</u> flour; 340 ml should be enough. Gently heat 118 ml of milk to a <u>lukewarm</u> temperature. You can <u>substitute</u> water if necessary. Shake 5 ml of baking powder from its <u>canister</u> into the mixture. <u>Crush</u> 118 ml of walnuts and add. Pour the mixture into a baking pan. Sprinkle an assortment of colored candies on top. Bake at 350 degrees for one hour.

Directions: Circle each word's meaning as it is used in the recipe.

1. acquire
   A. criticize
   B. hand
   C. get
   D. match

2. dab
   A. a lot
   B. a little bit
   C. a panful
   D. a stick

3. critical
   A. angry
   B. necessary
   C. unimportant
   D. random

4. gadget
   A. tool
   B. type
   C. spoon
   D. fork

5. sufficient
   A. a lot
   B. a little
   C. too much
   D. enough

6. lukewarm
   A. cool
   B. tepid
   C. hot
   D. disinterested

7. substitute
   A. to replace with
   B. to continue
   C. to return
   D. to provide

8. canister
   A. box
   B. container
   C. crate
   D. flat

9. crush
   A. chop finely
   B. squeeze
   C. crowded
   D. slice

The Amazing Amadeus

Can you imagine a five-year-old composing music and then playing it on a child-sized violin? This was a part of the childhood of Wolfgang Amadeus Mozart, a young genius who grew up to be one of the most creative composers of all time. He was born in Salzburg, Austria, in January of 1756. His father, Leopold, was himself a composer and musician, so it was not long before he began to realize the giftedness of his son.

With his father and his older sister, Anna Maria, Mozart toured the royal courts of Europe, playing concerts for kings, queens, and the nobility. Leopold devoted most of his time to the careers of his children, who were both child prodigies. But Wolfgang Amadeus Mozart was remarkable. He could listen to any piece of music once and then play it from memory. He could play the keyboard or the violin blindfolded. Music that Mozart wrote at the age of five was as good as works by many adult composers of the time.

As an adult, Mozart earned his living by selling his compositions, giving concerts, and providing music lessons to the wealthy. None of these ventures earned him much money, and he spent far more than he was able to earn. He was always in debt.

When Mozart was a young man, he fell in love with a German singer, a woman named Aloysia Weber. He wanted to give up his career to help hers, but his parents forbade it. Mozart postponed his wedding plans, and when he tried to return to the relationship, Alyosia spurned him. Instead, Mozart married her younger sister, Constanze Weber. His family did not approve of this marriage either. The young couple never had much money, but they were devoted to each other. They loved to attend parties and balls.

To earn money, Mozart wrote operas. Some of his most famous works were *The Marriage of Figaro*, *The Magic Flute*, and *Don Giovanni*, all of which are still performed today. Mozart also wrote music for the court of the Emperor of Austria. He composed 41 symphonies, works of three or four movements performed by an orchestra. Mozart often waited until the last moment to work on pieces that had been commissioned, or paid for in advance. For example, he did not write the overture to *Don Giovanni* until the night before it was going to be performed!

By the spring of 1791, Mozart was ill and depressed. He was deeply in debt. His health, which had never been good, was declining. He was visited by a stranger who asked Mozart to write a *requiem*, a musical work for a funeral. Mozart agreed to take the commission, but then he began to fear that the requiem was actually being written for his own death. Unfortunately, his fears were justified. Mozart died in December of 1791, at the age of 35.

The Amazing Amadeus (cont.)

Directions: Circle the correct answer for each question. Then write a summary of the article.

1. The *Amazing Amadeus* is—

    A. autobiography.

    B. biography.

    C. fiction.

    D. a ballad.

2. A prodigy is—

    A. a young person who plays the violin.

    B. a young person who shows exceptional   talent.

    C. a young person who studies music.

    D. a young person who likes music.

3. Mozart's father, a composer, was named—

    A. Amadeus.

    B. Constanze.

    C. Leopold.

    D. Aloysia.

4. Which one of these is an opera by Mozart?

    A. *La Bohéme*

    B. *Turandot*

    C. *Don Giovanni*

    D. *Carmen*

5. How many symphonies did Mozart compose?

    A. 35

    B. 41

    C. 40

    D. 13

6. What can you tell about Mozart's personality from this biography?

    A. He was serious and hardworking.

    B. He was irresponsible with money and in poor health.

    C. He was careful, thoughtful, and studious.

    D. He was angry and aggressive.

7. Write a summary of the biography. Try to include at least one sentence about each paragraph.

    _____

    _____

    _____

    _____

    _____

    _____

    _____

     © Carson-Dellosa

◆◇◆◇◆◇◆◇◆◇◆◇◆◇◆◇◆◇◆◇◆◇◆◇◆◇◆◇◆◇◆◇◆

A Soldier with a Secret

Union flag   Confederate flag

Among the hundreds of Civil War soldiers buried in Chalmette National Cemetery lies one soldier with a tombstone that reads "Lyons Wakeman, N.Y." If you researched Lyons Wakeman, you might think at first that he was an ordinary soldier of the time. He wrote home to his parents, telling about battles and marches. He described what it was like to march 200 miles in ten days, and how it felt to experience the heat and humidity of the South for the first time. In one letter, he wrote, "I don't know how long before I shall have to go into the field of battle. For my part, I don't care. I don't feel afraid to go." The soldier did not die from a wound in battle, but from a lengthy illness in 1864.

For years, his New York family did not speak much of Lyons Wakeman. It was not until a great-nephew found the soldier's letters that a well-kept secret was revealed: Lyons was actually a woman. Her name was Sarah Rosetta Wakeman. Her parents, ashamed of Rosetta's "unfeminine" nature, had hidden her letters and tried to allow her younger siblings to forget about her. Rosetta had served in the military and was buried in a soldier's grave without her secret ever being revealed to those who knew her as a private in the Army. And she was not alone. Research has shown that at least 400 women dressed as men to serve in the war, and there may have been many more. These women had different reasons for joining the Army. Some wanted to be with husbands or brothers. Some wanted to fight for the cause of freeing the slaves or protecting the Confederacy. Some wanted adventure.

Rosetta was born in 1843, the first child of a large farming family. Her letters reveal that she wanted to earn more money for her financially struggling family. She left home in August of 1862 and found work on a coal barge. She wrote home and sent part of her pay with every letter. On a trip up the river, Rosetta met a group of soldiers from the 153rd Regiment of New York State Volunteers. They encouraged the "boatman" to enlist. Rosetta was paid an enlistment bonus of $152, which was more than a year's wages for most men of the time. She continued to send home her Army pay until her death, and her reports to her parents speak of her pride in being able to drill, march, and fight as well as any man with whom she served.

If you are thinking that someone should have noticed that Rosetta was short, beardless, and had a higher voice than most men, you are both right and wrong. Rosetta was described in her enlistment papers as being "five feet tall, fair complected, with brown hair, blue eyes, and an occupation of boatman." By the time Rosetta enlisted, the army was routinely accepting younger men and even boys. Smooth skin, shortness, and higher voices were common and gave no cause for suspicion. If her fellow soldiers thought that "Lyon" had a secret, they would assume he was a young teen who had lied about his age...not that she was a farm girl who had decided to earn a man's wages.

The Civil War was full of tragic losses and stories of bravery on both sides of the battle. Perhaps more stories will come to light about the special bravery of women like Rosetta who were determined to fight alongside men in this historic struggle.

A Soldier with a Secret (cont.)

Directions: Circle **Yes** or **No** to answer each question. Then write a summary of the article.

1. *A Soldier with a Secret* is the autobiography of Sarah Rosetta Wakeman.

   Yes   No

2. Lyons Wakeman was Rosetta's brother.

   Yes   No

3. Rosetta's main reason for enlisting was to free the slaves.

   Yes   No

4. As a boatman, Rosetta was paid a $152 bonus by the Army.

   Yes   No

5. Rosetta is buried as a soldier in Chalmette National Cemetery.

   Yes   No

6. Sarah Rosetta Wakeman was the only female soldier in the Civil War.

   Yes   No

7. Write a summary of the events of Sarah Rosetta Wakeman's life. Be sure to include any details of her early life and her reasons for leaving home.

   _____

   _____

   _____

   _____

   _____

A Hidden Wonder

The black, funnel-shaped cloud rising every day at sunset in the Chihuahuan Desert went largely ignored for thousands of years. Native Americans noticed it, but did not record any attempts to track its source. Cowboys in the region thought the cloud was smoke pouring from the earth, and avoided it.

In June of 1901, however, a teenaged cowboy named Jim White happened to see the large, black cloud as it poured out of the earth. He was curious and went to investigate. Instead of finding a volcano, as he had imagined, he discovered something equally amazing. It was a billowing mass of bats! Numbering in the millions, the bats flew out of a hole in the ground to go on their nighttime hunts for food. Jim White was the first known person in this remote area of New Mexico who saw the flight of the bats at close hand.

After the bats had flown away that evening, Jim crawled bravely down the gaping hole. It was pitch black, but Jim could sense that the tunnel led somewhere. Two days later, he returned with a lantern to explore further. The hole actually opened into two tunnels. One was obviously the home of the bats, and Jim decided to explore the second tunnel instead. It opened up into magnificent cave rooms filled with gigantic calcite formations. Jim was awestruck and explored so long that his lantern went out. He managed to refill it with just enough kerosene to find his way back to the entrance.

The next time Jim White went to the cave, he brought a friend and supplies. They explored for three days and returned with descriptions that were so fantastic that few people believed them. The cowboys on nearby ranches and the people in the tiny town of Carlsbad treated Jim's stories as tall tales and nothing more.

After years of exploring the caves and finding no one to believe his stories, Jim White decided to create his own tourist attraction. He built trails and installed railings along the paths he had found. One day in 1915, two men asked Jim for a tour. After seeing the incredible caves, the men returned with a professional photographer named Ray V. Davis. Local doubts were finally put to rest by the photographs of the hidden beauty that Jim had discovered. All 13 residents of Carlsbad finally took a tour of the caves, which came to be known as Carlsbad Caverns.

In 1923, the government sent an inspector named Robert Holly to tour the caves. Later that year, the caverns were declared a national monument, and in 1930 they became a national park. Jim White lived to see the Carlsbad Caverns become world-famous. Today, tourists can hike to and tour some of the 100 known caves in this huge natural wonder, thanks to the persistence and dedication of one cowboy from New Mexico.

◆◆◆◆◆◆◆◆◆◆◆◆◆◆◆◆◆◆◆◆◆◆◆◆◆◆◆◆◆◆◆◆◆◆◆

A Hidden Wonder (cont.)

Directions: Write answers to each question.

1. Is *A Hidden Wonder* a biography or autobiography? How do you know?

   _____

   _____

   _____

2. Rewrite this sentence so it could be part of an autobiography of Jim White: "In June of 1901, a young teenaged cowboy named Jim White happened to see the large, black cloud as it poured out of the earth."

   _____

   _____

   _____

3. Describe one of the main differences between a biography and an autobiography.

   _____

   _____

4. Write a sentence that could be part of a biography about Ray V. Davis.

   _____

   _____

Directions: Put these events in Jim White's life in order by writing 1 through 7 in the blanks.

_____ Jim White takes Ray V. Davis into the caves.

_____ Jim decides to build paths and install railings in the caves.

_____ Jim White sees a black cloud rising from a hole in the ground.

_____ Jim spends three days exploring the caves with a friend.

_____ The residents of Carlsbad finally tour the caves with Jim White.

_____ Carlsbad Caverns are declared a national park.

_____ Carlsbad Caverns are declared a national monument.

The Young Life of Frederick Douglass

I have never met with a slave who could tell me how old he was. Few slave-mothers know anything of the months of the year, nor of the days of the month. They keep no family records, with marriages, births, and deaths. They measure the ages of their children by spring time, winter time, harvest time, planting time, but these soon become undistinguishable and forgotten. Like other slaves, I cannot tell how old I am. This destitution was among my earliest troubles. I learned when I grew up that my master—and this is the case with masters generally—allowed no questions to be put to him, by which a slave might learn his age. Such questions are deemed evidence of impatience, and even of impudent curiosity. From certain events, however, the dates of which I have since learned, I suppose myself to have been born about the year 1817.

…The dwelling of my grandmother and grandfather had few pretensions. It was a log hut, or cabin, built of clay, wood, and straw. At a distance it resembled—although it was much smaller, less commodious, and less substantial—the cabins erected in the western states by the first settlers. To my child's eye, however, it was a noble structure, admirably adapted to promote the comforts and conveniences of its inmates. A few rough, Virginia fence-rails, flung loosely over the rafters above, answered the triple purpose of floors, ceilings, and bedsteads. To be sure, this upper apartment was reached only by a ladder—but what in the world for climbing could be better than a ladder? To me, this ladder was really a high invention, and possessed a sort of charm as I played with delight upon the rounds of it. In this little hut there was a large family of children; I dare not say how many. My grandmother—whether because too old for field service, or because she had so faithfully discharged the duties of her station in early life, I

know not—enjoyed the high privilege of living in a cabin, separate from the quarter, with no other burden than her own support, and the necessary care of the little children, imposed. She evidently esteemed it a great fortune to live so. The children were not her own, but her grandchildren—the children of her daughters. She took delight in having them around her, and in attending to their few wants.…

Living here, with my dear old grandmother and grandfather, it was a long time before I knew myself to be a slave. I knew many other things before I knew that. Grandmother and Grandfather were the greatest people in the world to me; and being with them so snugly in their own little cabin, knowing no higher authority over me…for a time there was nothing to disturb me. But as I grew larger and older, I learned by degrees the sad fact that the "little hut" and the lot on which it stood, belonged not to my dear old grandparents, but to some person who lived a great distance off, and who was called by Grandmother, "Old Master." I further learned the sadder fact that not only the house and lot, but that Grandmother herself (Grandfather was free) and all the little children around her, belonged to this mysterious personage.

Excerpted from *My Bondage and My Freedom* by Frederick Douglass

◆◆

The Young Life of Frederick Douglass (cont.)

Directions: Fill in the blanks to complete each sentence.

1. *My Bondage and My Freedom* is an _____ written by Frederick Douglass.

2. Douglass describes his early life, when he lived in a _____ with his grandparents.

3. Douglass describes a _____ as a "high invention" that he loved to play upon.

4. Because he lived with his grandparents, Douglass did not realize at first that he was a _____.

5. Eventually, Douglass realized that his grandmother, the children, and her cabin were all owned by someone called _____.

6. Douglass's grandfather was not a slave, but a _____ man.

7. Douglass's grandmother had two duties: to take care of herself and to take care of her _____.

8. Because slave mothers did not keep track of months and years, few slaves knew in what year or month they were _____.

9. Douglass thought that he had been born sometime around _____.

10. One way that a reader can tell this is an autobiography is that the work is written in _____ person.

Directions: Write two or three sentences to start your own autobiography.

11. _____

    _____

    _____

    _____

When Lightning Strikes

What was Benjamin Franklin thinking when he flew a kite in a thunderstorm? Didn't he realize that his kite could attract a lightning bolt capable of killing him? The Philadelphia inventor was actually very lucky. A bolt of lightning heats the surrounding air to a temperature that is five times the heat on the surface of the sun. Yet the charge is so brief that people can sometimes survive a stroke of lightning. The bolt that hit Franklin's kite was weak. It struck a pointed wire attached to the kite, traveled down the kite string, and ignited a spark at the key that was fastened to the end of the string. With this experiment, Franklin proved that lightning is actually electricity.

Later in his life, Franklin invented the lightning rod, a device that sends lightning's electricity from a rod to a cable in the ground. Lightning rods are still in use today, and are especially handy in places like Florida, where 90 lightning-producing storms hit per year. By contrast, the West Coast receives an average of only three thunderstorms per year.

When a thunderstorm hits, don't be outdoors flying a kite! In fact, it's dangerous to be outdoors at all. The best place to be is inside a building. When lightning strikes a house, it travels through the wires inside the house and then goes into the ground. People in the house are usually protected. People in cars are also fairly safe. If lightning strikes a vehicle, the charge usually travels through the metal frame, bypassing the people inside. If you get caught outdoors, stay away from trees—lightning will strike the tallest object. It's better to crouch in a ditch or a low spot in the land. Stay away from tents, unwired buildings such as old barns, and shallow caves. Bodies of water should also be avoided during a thunderstorm.

Lightning literally bombards the Earth; there are more than 100 lightning strikes every second. In the United States, more people are killed by lightning than by tornadoes or hurricanes. However, nearly twice as many people who are struck by lightning survive than die. Some people have even survived multiple lightning strikes, such as Virginia park ranger Roy C. Sullivan. He has been struck by lightning seven times.

So, is lightning nothing but menacing? Actually, lightning plays an important part in the balance of nature. It returns negative energy to the Earth and produces nitrogen compounds that are important for plants. There is no reason to panic over lightning. The chances of being killed by a lightning strike are less than one in 2.5 million. So the next time there's a thunderstorm, put away your kite, find a safe place, and enjoy one of nature's most dramatic shows.

When Lightning Strikes (cont.)

Directions: Write an answer for each question.

1. Describe what *When Lightning Strikes* is about.

   _____

   _____

2. For what audience did the author write this selection?

   _____

   _____

3. Why do you think that the author started the article with a reference to Benjamin Franklin?

   _____

   _____

4. Does the author present both the negative and positive aspects of lightning? Give examples.

   _____

   _____

5. Why does the author end the article with a reference to a kite?

   _____

   _____

6. What is the author's purpose in presenting safety tips concerning thunderstorms?

   _____

   _____

7. What does the author say are your chances of being killed by lightning?

   _____

   _____

8. Is the author's purpose in writing this selection to entertain, to inform, or to persuade?

   _____

   _____

Golden Words

Rose O'Neal Greenhow sighed. She picked up the pen and leaned forward, writing the secretary of state's address at the top of a sheet of stationery. She had just begun the letter that she hoped would result in her freedom.

She protested that she had been unfairly imprisoned. Jailers held her and her daughter in Washington's Old Capitol Prison. "And thus for a period of seven days, I, with my little child, was placed absolutely at the mercy of men without character or responsibility," Greenhow wrote in her 1861 letter.

People usually paid attention to Greenhow. Nicknamed "Wild Rose" when she was still a child, she grew up to be a famous Washington hostess. As the Civil War loomed, she spoke often and passionately about her views. She opposed Lincoln's decisions.

When war broke out, Greenhow did not stop talking. She just did it in secret. She worked with devious skill as a Confederate spy. Her position as hostess put her in contact with many important people, and she used her charm and position to obtain and overhear information. So important was the information she leaked that some historians credit her with two important Confederate victories early in the war. She managed to get information to the Confederates even after her imprisonment, hiding messages in women visitors' hair and other unlikely places.

Greenhow's letter did not win her immediate release, but she was eventually let out of prison. She was exiled to the Confederacy. From there she traveled to England, where she used her skill with words to drum up sympathy for treacherous Confederate causes. She also wrote her prison memoirs, and her publishers paid her in gold.

Those golden words proved to be her undoing. When she was returning from England on the *Condor*, a Union gunboat pursued the vessel. The *Condor* ran aground. Greenhow escaped in a rowboat, but that boat capsized. The weight of the gold she was carrying in her clothing dragged Greenhow down. She drowned, killed by the weight of her own words.

◆✕◆

Golden Words (cont.)

Directions: Write an answer to each question.

1. Sometimes an author will appear to write a factual article, but the work either does not present all viewpoints or it uses words and phrases to bias the reader. Find and write down four adjectives or phrases that the author uses in *Golden Words* to influence the reader's opinion.

   _____

   _____

   _____

   _____

   ___

2. The author could have written the article without including Greenhow's nickname. Why do you think the author included this detail?

   _____

   _____

3. Why do you think that the author chose to add the detail that it was the weight of Greenhow's payment in gold that contributed to her death?

   _____

   _____

4. How does your impression of Greenhow's imprisonment change from the beginning to the end of the article? Why does it change?

   _____

   _____

   _____

5. In your opinion, does the author want you to admire Greenhow's courage or to feel that Greenhow's defiance led to her own death? Support your opinion with examples from the article.

   _____

   _____

   _____

   _____

   ___

Doctor Anna

Anna Pierce Hobbs Bigsby was one determined woman.

In the early nineteenth century, women performed most of the nursing at home for their own family members, but Bigsby wanted to do more than nurse. Born in 1808, she had become a pioneer at the age of 16 when her family moved to Illinois. The wilderness of Illinois had few doctors, and Anna wanted to serve her community. But in the nineteenth century, few medical schools admitted women. When Anna finally located a school in Philadelphia, the school limited the courses that she could take. Fortunately, no school could limit her curiosity and determination.

When Doctor Anna, as she came to be known, returned home in 1828, she soon faced an epidemic that was sweeping through southern Illinois. Both people and animals were the victims of a mysterious illness called "milk sickness." They walked stiffly, trembled, and became increasingly weak. Many died. Anna lost her mother and sister-in-law to milk sickness. Another resident of Illinois, Abraham Lincoln, lost his mother in this same epidemic.

Many settlers blamed witches for the illness, but Doctor Anna set aside this ridiculous explanation. She was determined to use her medical training to find the true cause of the disease. Her notes soon revealed that milk sickness became serious in the summer, and then abated after the first frost in the autumn. Although horses, goats, and pigs sometimes were affected, cattle were the most frequent animal victims. Doctor Anna wondered if something that the cattle ate caused the illness. She also noted that people might be contracting the illness from drinking tainted milk or eating tainted meat from the cattle.

Anna began doing field work in the truest sense of the word: she headed to the fields

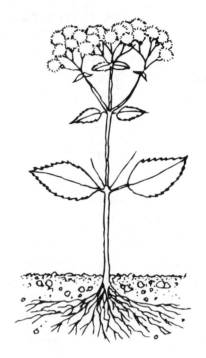

and observed grazing cattle. One day when she was following a herd, she met a Shawnee woman. As they talked, the Shawnee woman showed the doctor a plant called white snakeroot. The Native American suggested that this poisonous plant might be causing the problem.

Doctor Anna set up an experiment to test the Shawnee woman's theory. After feeding white snakeroot to a calf, she was able to prove that the plant caused milk sickness. Then this energetic doctor began a campaign to convince farmers in the area to get rid of the plants. As a result, many lives were saved.

Most resources do not list Doctor Anna's discovery of the source of milk sickness. At the time of her death in 1869, neither Anna nor the anonymous Shawnee woman had received any credit for this important medical breakthrough. But Doctor Anna had been determined to stop people from dying of milk sickness, and that is exactly what she achieved.

Doctor Anna (cont.)

Directions: Write an answer to each question.

1. Through word choices, authors can suggest a certain image of a person about whom they are writing. What word is most often used to describe Doctor Anna?

   _____

2. List two other words that are used to describe Anna's character and personality.

   _____

3. What unstated beliefs might the author have about nineteenth-century women's difficulties in attending medical school? Give a specific example to support your answer.

   _____

   _____

   _____

4. The author does not specifically say why Doctor Anna suspected a food source as the cattle's illness. How does the author imply this?

   _____

   _____

5. The author writes that Doctor Anna did not believe the ridiculous theory that witches were causing milk sickness. Whose opinion is it that this was a ridiculous theory?

   _____

6. Using the information in the reading selection, write a brief biographical summary of Doctor Anna's life. Do not include any opinions of your own.

   _____

   _____

   _____

   _____

   _____

Contemplating Color

It's 101 degrees outside and your house doesn't have air conditioning. Do you dive into a pool? Do you drink glass after glass of ice water? You might want to sit very quietly in a room that is painted blue. Scientific studies have shown that people feel cooler in blue rooms than in a room that is painted red or pink. This fact could explain why, over centuries of time, different colors have been used to symbolize human emotions or characteristics. Perhaps our physical reaction to color has helped explain how these symbols came to be. The color blue causes people to relax and their heart rates to slow down. Blue has often been used to symbolize tranquility and calm. But it also is linked with depression, or "the blues." That's because that blue room might be a peaceful haven for a time, but if you spend too much time there, you can start feeling depressed or sad.

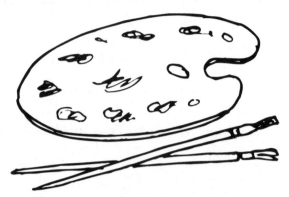

Let's look at red. All you have to do is think of Valentine's Day to know that red symbolizes love and passion in Western culture. But did you know that the color red actually speeds up a person's breathing and increases the heart rate? That reaction could be the very thing that linked the color and the emotion of falling in love in the first place.

When you think of purple, do you think of royalty? For centuries, purple was the color of kings and queens. There was a practical reason for this originally: purple was the most costly of all dyes, and only those with tremendous wealth could afford purple cloth. In color studies, purple has been found to be the favorite color of people who are creative and intuitive—qualities that the best of rulers have had in both history and legend. So again, there may be a physical, scientific link to the ongoing symbol.

Black is another color with strong symbolism. In Western culture, we associate it with death, mystery, and evil. Black is the color that Europeans have used for mourning. In the nineteenth century, people whose spouse or child died were expected to wear black clothing for a set period of time to symbolize their loss. Farther back in time, we find black associated with evil, perhaps because it is also the color that represents night, a time when people were frightened of attacks, robberies, or even a visit from a ghost or witch.

Green is a color we associate with nature, springtime, and fertility. In medieval Europe, brides used to wear green dresses to show their hope that they would have many children. It's not surprising that we link green with nature; when you look outside, green is one of the most prominent colors in most natural settings. And the healing properties of nature convey themselves through the color green—it has a healing and soothing effect on people who are ill, which is why many hospitals choose the color for patients' rooms.

Symbols concerning color have ancient roots. When we look at the scientific and cultural links to various colors, suddenly the symbolism itself makes more sense.

◆◇◆◇◆◇◆◇◆◇◆◇◆◇◆◇◆◇◆◇◆◇◆◇◆◇◆◇◆◇◆◇◆◇◆◇

Contemplating Color (cont.)

Directions: Fill in the chart. For number 6, choose another color and decide on its symbolism and where it could be used.

Color	Symbol	Use
1. blue		
2. red	love and passion	
3. green		hospital rooms
4. black		
5. purple		
6.		

7.   What color would you paint an art classroom? Why?

_____

_____

8.   If you were making a banner to symbolize a new beginning, what color would you make it? Why?

_____

_____

9.   What is your favorite color? Why?

_____

_____

Lincoln's Dream

About ten days ago, I retired very late. I had been up waiting for important dispatches from the front. I could not have been long in bed when I fell into a slumber, for I was weary. I soon began to dream. There seemed to be a death-like stillness about me. Then I heard subdued sobs, as if a number of people were weeping. I thought I left my bed and wandered downstairs. There the silence was broken by the same pitiful sobbing, but the mourners were invisible. I went from room to room; no living person was in sight, but the same mournful sounds of distress met me as I passed along. I saw light in all the rooms; every object was familiar to me; but where were all the people who were grieving as if their hearts would break? I was puzzled and alarmed. What could be the meaning of all this? Determined to find the cause of a state of things so mysterious and so shocking, I kept on until I arrived at the East Room, which I entered. There I met with a sickening surprise. Before me was a catafalque, on which rested a corpse wrapped in funeral vestments. Around it were stationed soldiers who were acting as guards; and there was a throng of people, gazing mournfully upon the corpse, whose face was covered, others weeping pitifully. "Who is dead in the White House?" I demanded of one of the soldiers.

"The President," was his answer; "he was killed by an assassin." Then came a loud burst of grief from the crowd, which woke me from my dream. I slept no more that night; and although it was only a dream, I have been strangely annoyed by it ever since.

—Account of a dream of Abraham Lincoln's. It was written down by Ward Hill Lamon, who heard President Lincoln give this account to a group of friends a few days before he went to Ford's Theater to see *Our American Cousin*.

Lincoln's Dream (cont.)

Directions: Circle the correct answer.

1. Foreshadowing is an indication of something that is going to happen. What event does Lincoln's dream foreshadow?

   A. the death of John F. Kennedy

   B. Lincoln's own assassination

   C. the death of Lincoln's son

   D. the death of Lincoln's wife

2. How long before his assassination did Lincoln have this dream?

   A. about ten days before

   B. about three days before

   C. about two weeks before

   D. about one month before

3. Which elements of this dream indicate foreshadowing?

   A. Lincoln had been waiting for reports from the front.

   B. Lincoln sees a corpse which soldiers tell him is the body of the President.

   C. All of the rooms are lighted and familiar-looking.

   D. Lincoln sees the spirit of his dead son in the East Room.

4. Dreams are one type of foreshadowing. Which of these would be another type of foreshadowing?

   A. someone feeling a sudden chill right before hearing bad news

   B. a dog barking without any reason

   C. a mother warning a child to dress warmly for school

   D. All of the above.

5. *Lincoln's Dream* is from a historical account. Which of these is a foreshadowing event in fiction?

   A. Hansel and Gretel arrive at the witch's house.

   B. The ghost of Hamlet's father warns Hamlet about his uncle.

   C. Laura Ingalls Wilder moves to Dakota Territory with her family.

   D. Oliver Twist learns from Fagin how to pick pockets.

6. Write the first few sentences of a story about a boy who becomes lost in a snowstorm. Include an element of foreshadowing.

   _____

   _____

   _____

   _____

Dick Turpin's Ride

"Dick Turpin, bold Dick, hie away," was the cry
Of my pals, who were startled, you guess.
The pistols were leveled, the bullets whizzed by,
As I jumped on the back of Black Bess.

Three officers, mounted, led forward the chase,
Resolved in the capture to share;
But I smiled on their efforts, though swift was their pace,
As I urged on my bonny black mare.

"Hark away, hark away!" Still onward we press,
And I saw by the glimmers of morn,
Full many a mile on the back of Black Bess
That night I was gallantly borne.

When the spires of York Minister now burst on my view,
And the chimes they are ringing a knell—
"Halt, halt! my brave mare, they no longer pursue."
As she halted, she staggered, she fell.

Her breathings are over, all hushed to her grave,
My poor Black Bess, once my pride.
But her heart she had burst, her rider to save—
For Dick Turpin she lived and she died.

                        Anonymous 19th century poem

Dick Turpin's Ride (cont.)

Directions: Circle the correct answer.

1. What is this poem about?

   A. A man is captured and killed.

   B. A man rides his horse to death.

   C. Officers ride their horses to death.

   D. A pursuit by officers leads to an arrest.

2. What detail of the poem foreshadows a death?

   A. the friends calling out warnings to Dick Turpin

   B. the glimmer of morning on the horizon

   C. the bells ringing a knell, which is done for funerals

   D. the horse's breathing coming to an end

3. What is York Minister?

   A. a graveyard

   B. a boat

   C. a farm

   D. a church

4. Dick Turpin was a real-life *highwayman*, a robber of stagecoaches. How can you tell in the poem that he is a criminal?

   A. He rides a fast horse.

   B. He rides his horse to death.

   C. He is being chased by officers.

   D. His friends are shooting at him.

5. How would you characterize Dick Turpin's feelings about his horse?

   A. He didn't care about her, even when she died.

   B. He loved her and admired the sacrifice she made for him.

   C. He was proud of how fast she could run.

   D. He had no particular feelings for her.

6. If this poem had been about Dick Turpin's arrest, what event might foreshadow that?

   A. Dick shoots and kills one of the officers chasing him.

   B. Dick falls off his horse and the officers catch up to him.

   C. Dick imagines he sees an officer in front of him, but it turns out to be a tree.

   D. Dick thinks back to a time when he was a soldier himself.

Venice

Just before my family left on this trip, we bought a new television. A man from the store drove to our house in a van to deliver it. Today, in Venice, I watched a family bring home a new television set to their house. They had purchased it on the mainland. Then they hired a *wherry*—a narrow rowboat—to bring them and their new set back home. When they got to the entrance of the narrow canal where they lived, the boat docked, and the family had to carry the set down the walkway to their house.

People don't live in this city because it is modern or convenient. They live here because of its strange beauty. The network of canals and sidewalks is complicated and the water carries noises from a long distance. But around every corner is a wonderful surprise: an ancient sculpture, an old church, or a designer dress shop in which you can spend a few hours.

Cars don't exist here. There are no roads. The canals provide the venue for transportation, which is mostly by *gondolas* and *vaporettos*. The gondolas are lightweight, narrow barges that look like large canoes but serve as taxis. The *gondoliers*, professional boat operators, propel and steer these boats with single paddles. The first time I rode in a gondola, I was nervous, but only for a few minutes. Our gondolier sang and joked with us as he maneuvered our gondola through the crowded canal. I've also ridden on a *vaporetto*, a water bus. It's faster and more efficient, but it's not nearly as romantic! Vaporettos travel from station to station, just like regular city buses. When you get off the water bus, you walk…and walk, and walk! There are narrow pathways and hundreds of bridges to span the canals.

Nothing prepared me for the majesty of this city. The rows of curving buildings rise up from the canals as they have for centuries. The baroque churches tower over the smaller townhouses. Scattered boat launches and porches open right onto the water, which gives the appearance of a city filled with flooded streets. In fact, Venice was first built more than 1,000 years ago on a series of 118 islands that filled the great Lagoon of Venice. The first residents made their living by fishing in the muddy marshland. Over the centuries, from these humble beginnings grew this jewel of Italy, a city like no other on earth. I love to imagine all of the people who have traveled on these canals.

Venice (cont.)

Directions: Circle the correct answer.

1. In what point of view is *Venice* written?

   A. first person

   B. second person

   C. third person

2. If this article had been written in third-person, it would most resemble—

   A. a personal account of traveling in the city.

   B. a factual account of the city of Venice and its history.

   C. a review of a good hotel in Venice.

3. Who is the most likely speaker in this story?

   A. a travel agent who is recommending Venice to his customers

   B. a student traveling with her family in Italy

   C. a schoolteacher guiding a group of students in Venice

4. How do you know that the speaker appreciates Venice?

   A. The speaker talks of the city's strange beauty

   B. The speaker talks of spending a few hours in a dress shop.

   C. The speaker talks of new television sets.

5. What is a vaporetto?

   A. a canoe-like taxi

   B. a barge for carrying goods

   C. a water bus

6. What is the most unusual aspect of Venice?

   A. It has ancient churches.

   B. It has canals instead of streets.

   C. It was built more than 1,000 years ago.

7. How does the speaker first establish the difference between Venice and other cities?

   A. by describing how a family has to bring home a television

   B. by describing the gondolas and vaporettos

   C. by describing the history of Venice

8. How do you know that the speaker does not live in Venice?

   A. She says in the first sentence that she and her family are on a trip there.

   B. She is nervous the first time she gets into a gondola.

   C. A and B

9. Would you like to live in Venice? Give reasons for your answer.

   _____

   _____

   _____

   _____

The Baseball Card

I have to keep my hand from shaking, thought Mark as he picked up the baseball card. Suddenly, the air in the swap meet seemed too warm. He stared at the early twentieth-century image and then slowly turned the card over.

"That's one of my favorites," said the elderly man. "My dad got that in a pack of gum when he was a boy."

"How…how much?" asked Mark. He cleared his voice.

The man thought for a minute. "Fifty dollars," he said. Then he bit his lip. Maybe it was too much to ask, especially from a boy.

Mark felt his head swimming. The baseball card was in perfect condition. It showed the open, friendly face of Honus Wagner, a player from the Pittsburgh Pirates. Wagner had played with the Pirates until the outbreak of World War I. Nearly 20 years later, he had been one of the first players inducted into the Baseball Hall of Fame. Mark looked at the old man and knew he did not realize what a treasure he had.

The man watched Mark as he studied the card. I sure could use that $50, the man thought. He would settle for $40, but he wanted to see what the boy would say first.

Mark looked at the man's face and the frayed collar of his shirt. I've never seen him at one of these swap meets before, thought Mark. I bet he is here because he needs some money, not because he knows a lot about baseball cards. Mark closed his eyes for a moment. What do I do? he asked himself. If I made this trade, it would be the biggest thing that ever happened to me. But I would have to remember that I robbed this man for the rest of my life.

The man looked at the boy hopefully, and then his heart sank as Mark shook his head and handed back the card. How will I pay for that prescription? he wondered.

Mark hesitated for a minute, and then he leaned forward. "Look," he said. "I know a lot about baseball cards. You should not be selling this card here. You need to take it to an antiques dealer." The man's eyes widened as Mark added, "That card is worth a lot more than $50. The last time a Honus Wagner card was sold, it made more than half a million dollars." Then the boy turned on his heel and walked away, before the old man could see the tears in Mark's eyes. Walking away was the hardest thing Mark had ever done in his life.

86

The Baseball Card (cont.)

Directions: Circle or write the correct answer.

1. From what point of view is *The Baseball Card* written?

   A. first person

   B. second person

   C. third person

2. Is this point of view omniscient or limited? Give an example to support your answer.

   _____

   _____

   _____

   _____

3. What is the first clue in the story that the baseball card is valuable?

   A. Mark recognizes that the card is of Honus Wagner.

   B. Mark tells himself that he has to keep his hand from shaking.

   C. Mark cannot look the old man in the eyes.

4. What is the old man's worry about Mark?

   A. Mark might not have enough money to pay for the card.

   B. Mark looks dishonest.

   C. Mark doesn't like the baseball card.

5. Describe Mark as a character. What are his main characteristics?

   _____

   _____

   _____

   _____

6. Describe the old man as a character. What are his main characteristics?

   _____

   _____

   _____

   _____

7. How would this story be different if you were unable to read the thoughts of the characters? What information would be missing?

   _____

   _____

   _____

   _____

   _____

   _____

   _____

   _____

A Letter Home

February 10, 1919

Dear Mother,

    Well, here I am in Archangel, and the temperature is about 30 below. Our commanding officer told us that Archangel is the largest city in the world so close to the Arctic Circle; it's only about 100 miles. I have no problem believing that. It seems as though we just stepped out of a time machine that has whisked us back to the Ice Age. How I miss Florida!

    After I finished my basic training, I was so sure that I would be sent overseas to fight the Germans. Shows how much I know. By the time our regiment reached France, the fighting was over, and we were ordered to Russia instead.

    It seems that here we've been sent into the middle of a civil war, which is still raging even though the Great War is over. I don't know how much of this you have read in the newspapers, but it's a mess. On one side are the White Russians. They are taking a heroic stand against the Bolsheviks (I hope I spelled that right). The Whites wanted to put the Tsar back on the throne. Now that the Tsar has been murdered, I'm not sure what the Whites would do if they won, but they are still fighting bravely. The Bolsheviks are called the Reds. They're the turncoats who made that deal with the Germans and backed out of the war.

    What am I doing here? Our job right now is to guard a heap of supplies that were left over after the Russians withdrew from the war. It seems the brass are worried that either the Bolsheviks or the Germans will try to grab them. So here I sit, babysitting a stockpile of bullets. Sometimes I wonder if we're also here just in case our government decides we need to step in and help the White Russians. But I'm afraid their cause is lost. From what I hear, Lenin has things pretty well under his thumb.

    How is Brad? Please tell him to write. It gets lonely standing guard and staring at nothing but snow. Speaking of which, it's time for me to go on duty. I'll write again in a few days.

Love,
Frank

A Letter Home (cont.)

Directions: Write answers to the questions.

1. From what point of view is this letter written?

   _____

   _____

   _____

2. Choose three adjectives to describe Frank, and explain why you chose them.

   _____

   _____

   _____

3. What words and phrases does Frank use to describe the White Russians that show his opinion of them?

   _____

   _____

   _____

4. What words and phrases does Frank use to describe the Red Russians, or Bolsheviks, that show his opinion of them?

   _____

   _____

   _____

5. Write a brief description of the events described in *A Letter Home*. Write the description using the third-person point of view.

   _____

   _____

   _____

In Another Country

Wesley Kidd and his family lived in Central America. Both of his parents were teachers in an English-speaking school. Wesley learned Spanish and made friends with many of the students at the school. The experience of being in another country was great. However, Wesley felt troubled for much of the two years he had lived there.

Much of what troubled Wesley was due to the economic hardships he observed in Central America. In most of the city in which he lived, the people were poor. Some of their homes were made from mud and bricks, while others lived in shacks of corrugated metal. Wesley saw the children from these homes walking back and forth from the community well all day, carrying water to their homes because they had no plumbing.

Before Wesley and his parents had moved to their Central American home, they had attended classes called "orientation workshops." They were told that the city they were moving to had many beggars. The orientation trainer warned them not to give the beggars money. "It doesn't teach these people how to be constructive members of society," she said. "And the beggars never learn how to be self-sufficient without charity. Sometimes they force their children to beg and they grow up knowing nothing else."

Still, Wesley wanted to do something to help the people who were less fortunate than he was. There was a little girl in a blue dress who sold flowers with her blind grandmother. The girl was only about six years old, and she seemed frail, even though she always smiled. Wesley bought flowers from them often, and brought the flowers home to give to his mother and sisters.

Wesley was most aware of the poverty in Central America when he and his parents would go out to eat in restaurants. Beggars would line up outside the restaurant, looking for leftover food from sympathetic diners. After seeing this, Wesley decided he could help by volunteering at a local food kitchen. It operated out of a church that was between his school and his house. The kitchen provided food and found employment opportunities for poor people.

Yesterday, Wesley learned that his parents have teaching jobs in the United States for the next school year. In a few short months, his family will be returning to their old home in Connecticut. Wesley is excited about seeing his grandparents and going to school again with his cousins. He knows he will miss the friends he made at the food kitchen, but he plans to make new friends at a volunteer food bank for poor people in Connecticut.

In Another Country (cont.)

Directions: Write answers to the questions.

1. Choose three words or phrases to describe Wesley.

   _____

   _____

2. What is Wesley's main concern since he has lived in Central America?

   _____

   _____

   _____

3. Do you think Wesley agreed or disagreed with the trainer in his orientation workshops? Give examples to support your answer.

   _____

   _____

   _____

   _____

4. What does Wesley see when he goes out to eat with his family?

   _____

   _____

   _____

   _____

5. If you were Wesley's older brother or sister, what suggestions would you make to help him with his concerns?

   _____

   _____

   _____

   _____

Geraldo's Journal

Our voyage has begun. I wish now that I had not signed on to this ship for this dreadful journey. All seemed well when we were loading our supplies and making the usual preparations. But now, a month later, I fear a curse has fallen over this ship. Only three days after we left, our mast was damaged. The *Santa María* and the *Niña* helped us get to port for repairs. The *Pinta* was seaworthy again after a few weeks. Now, we sail into the west day after day. The men whisper among themselves. They tell tales of terrible monsters who are waiting to devour our ship when we arrive at the edge of the ocean. I am fearful of these savage sea creatures, and just as fearful of the never-ending sea and the man who seems to believe we can find land where no land exists.

◆◆◆◆◆◆◆◆◆◆◆◆◆

Our situation worsens, but there may be a small hope of saving ourselves. For days now, the crew has grown more and more vocal about how long we have sailed without seeing anything but water, stretching in all directions. Finally, some of the older sailors went to Captain Pinzón with their fears. He spoke directly to the Lord Admiral himself. Afterward, our three ships changed direction to the southwest. I pray that this shift in direction will keep us from sailing off the edge of the world. A rumor has it that we will try this heading for

a few days only, and then turn back. I may never go to sea again, should I be fortunate enough to find my way safely home.

A miracle has occurred. Señor Cerdá saw a large piece of driftwood yesterday afternoon. Amid great excitement, Captain Pinzón examined it. He said that since the wood was not smooth, it could not have been in the water for long. Then, early this morning, the lookout on the *Santa María* spotted some birds. The crew did their work feverishly, scanning the horizon at every other moment. Finally, we heard our own lookout's cry, the one we had waited for every day. "Land! Land!" There it was, green and hazy on the horizon under a bank of low clouds. Not monsters, but land!

Name _____ Date _____

Geraldo's Journal (cont.)

Directions: Write answers to the questions.

1. This is a fictitious journal, but it describes a historic voyage. Choose three words or phrases to describe Geraldo, the fictitious seaman who is the "author" of the journal.

   _____

   _____

   _____

2. What are two of Geraldo's concerns on his sea voyage?

   _____

   _____

3. There are no dates on these journal entries. When were they written? How do you know?

   _____

   _____

   _____

4. Why were the birds and the driftwood so heartening to the crew?

   _____

   _____

5. Write two or three sentences to summarize what is going to happen to Geraldo and the rest of the crew after they land. What do they find? Do they get safely back home again?

   _____

   _____

   _____

6. Imagine that Geraldo goes back home after the adventure that is ahead of him. Do you think he will go back to sea again, as he wrote, or not? Give reasons for your answer.

   _____

   _____

   _____

The Dinner Party

Cleveland, Ohio
July 12, 1880

My Dear Grace,

Last night, Arthur and I had the honor of attending a dinner at the Rockefellers' home on Euclid Avenue. The common people of the town call this street "Millionaires' Row," and I must say the many mansions are impressive. But I admit that Mr. Rockefeller surprised me. Unlike other nabobs who go overboard to impress guests with their wealth, the celebrated John D. seems to be a genuinely simple man. A friend of mine told me that one of his favorite meals is bread and milk. Can you imagine that, Grace? This is a man who can afford any delicacy in the world, and he prefers bread and milk!

You and I have both heard the stories of the ruthless ways in which this man acquired his wealth, but after meeting him, I am skeptical. He was down-to-earth and amusing. I truly enjoyed meeting him.

Mr. Rockefeller talked to me during the soup course about his mother, speaking quite movingly about her religious faith and his admiration of the way she brought him up. Once, John and his brothers went skating on a frozen river, knowing full well that their mother had forbidden this and they would be punished if they were caught. While they were on the river, they saved the life of a boy who had fallen through the ice. Not bending an inch from her rules, their mother still punished them for their disobedience—although she did praise them for their heroic action first. He also told me that he made his first money raising turkeys, saving every penny after he sold the birds.

Later in the meal, one man who undoubtedly was trying to impress our host began a financial discussion that bored most of the guests to death. Our host, the richest man in the world, picked up a cracker and proceeded to balance it on the end of his nose! He grinned widely when he managed this trick on his first attempt. Everyone broke into laughter and applause.

The meal was excellent, but not lavish. So were our surroundings. The simplicity of the entertainment and the dinner was unexpected, but even more so was the simplicity and modesty of our host.

Please give my regards to all. I hope this letter finds you well, my dear friend. I will be home soon and will tell you more then.

Yours ever,
Ida

The Dinner Party (cont.)

Directions: Fill in the character web.

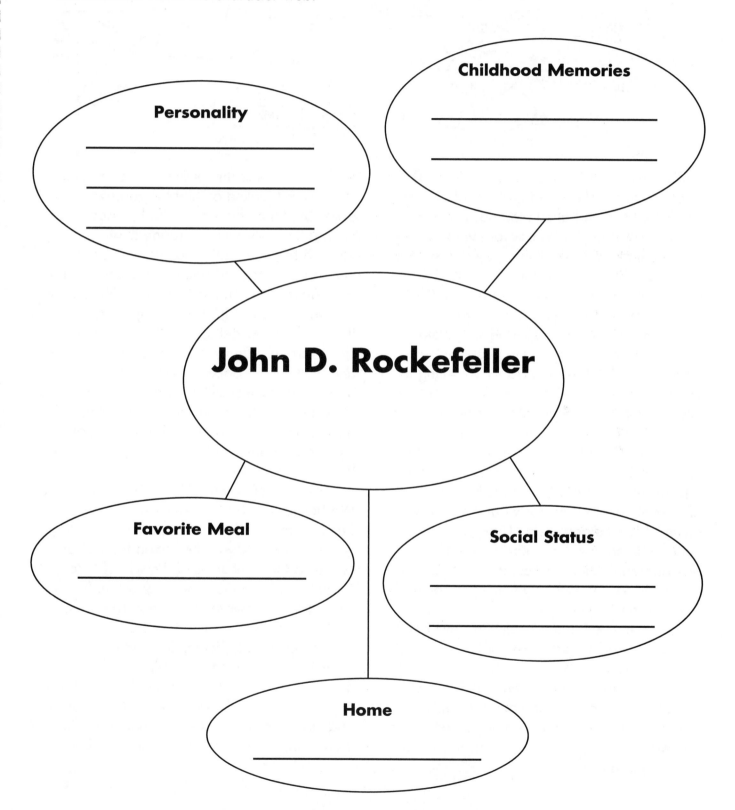

Personality

_____

_____

_____

Childhood Memories

_____

_____

John D. Rockefeller

Favorite Meal

_____

Social Status

_____

_____

Home

_____

Vacation

We were in school, but not in school. That is to say, our bodies were at our desks but our minds had traveled ahead to Friday. Friday was the last day of school before vacation. We stared out the window at the gray sky, sending all of our energy to the clouds. "Snow!" we commanded them. "Snow, please snow!"

At home, there were lots of secret conversations. Mom whispering to our big sister. Dad whispering on the phone to Grandma. We could also hear the rustling of wrapping paper coming from the home office. We knew there were packages somewhere in the house, gifts with our names on them, but my brother and I could not find them. So we sat in the living room, watching one silly holiday special after another. Out in the kitchen, pies were baking. Cookies were baking. The scents of vanilla and almonds tormented us. But everything was for Saturday, when the grandparents, aunts, uncles, and cousins would start arriving. I munched gloomily on some salty pretzels instead.

Under my bed, I had hidden my own gifts for everyone. I had saved money for weeks to buy my mother a soft, silky scarf. My brother was getting a computer game. I had made presents for some of my cousins and my grandmother. Late at night, I would gaze up at the clear, starry sky, waiting for the first snowflakes. It had not snowed yet that year.

Thursday was the longest day of my life. Every time I looked at the black-and-white clock, only a minute or two had passed since my last look. I fidgeted through English, yawned through math, tapped my fingers through science, and gnawed my pencil during a history test. Still no school bell. Still no snow.

On Friday, we had a holiday party in class. It was a relief to get up and move around. The classroom was decorated with giant snowflakes and white crêpe paper. This was ironic, because there was still no snow. I hovered near the windows, sipping my tart red punch and glancing outside. I pressed my hand against the windowpane. It felt cold enough to snow. Why wasn't it snowing?

The last bell sounded both shrill and sweet. We bolted into the hallways. My brother and I met up at the stairs. We charged down the green stairwell, down the brown-tiled lobby, and onto the front steps of the school. We stood there for a moment. Lazy, white flakes were drifting down from the sky. The grass was already wearing a white disguise.

I imagined our home, covered in snow, the windows glowing with yellow light. On Saturday, we would build snow forts and have a massive snowball battle, with all the cousins and several of the uncles. The house would glint in the sun, wearing its heavy cap of snow.

◆◆

Vacation (cont.)

Directions: Write answers to fill in the chart and answer the questions.

1. What are the two settings for this story?

   _____

   _____

   _____

2. Write a one-sentence description of each setting, based on details from the story.

   _____

   _____

   _____

3. In what month is this story probably set?

   _____

4. Write a two- to three-sentence description about the party that will occur on Saturday.

   _____

   _____

   _____

5. This story has many details that appeal to one of the five senses. Fill in the chart with two examples for each sense. The first one has been done for you.

	Detail 1	**Detail 2**
Sight	gray clouds	
Sound		
Taste		
Smell		
Touch		

In the Village

Have you ever wondered what a typical Incan farming village was like? Picture this: huge, snow-capped mountains tower over the small cluster of huts. The small, brown, grass-roofed huts in the village are made out of dried mud, called *adobe*.

The sleeping village wakes early, when the air flowing down from the mountains is still cold and blusters between the huts. Children go out to gather sticks to feed the fire, but there are few trees, so hunting for sticks is a challenge. The rough barking of dogs and the rumbling bray of the llamas can be heard in every hut. After a small meal, some villagers take their goats and sheep out to graze, while others go to work in the fields. Corn, potatoes, peanuts, and tomatoes are some of the main crops dotting the distant, terraced fields.

At midday, the main meal is prepared. A strong, bitter scent drifts from the clay jugs of *chicha*, a drink made from corn. It mixes with the spicy scent of guinea-pig stew cooking over the fire. Dried herbs and chilies are added to the stew as it cooks. As the sun reaches down to the little village, heavy woolen blankets as rough as dry grass are spread over stools or fences to dry and air out. Excitement spreads through the village at the sight of a *chasqui*, a messenger, who is carrying news and information from the cities to the smaller villages. Most of the villagers gather to hear what this visitor has to say.

In the evening, the distant cries of birds echo in the mountains. The last light illuminates the highest point in the village, kept for religious ceremonies because it is closest to the sun. As the light dies, the fires burn to red-gold embers and the people of the village go, one by one, to sleep.

In the Village (cont.)

Directions: For each one of the details of this setting, write the name of the sense it addresses and then a brief description of the detail. You may want to list more than one sense for certain details. The first one is done for you.

Thing	Sense	Description
1. huts	sight	small, brown, grass-roofed
2. mountains		
3. air		
4. animal noises		
5. blankets		
6. stew		
7. fields		
8. chicha		
9. birds		
10. fire		

11. Write a brief description of your room, using all five senses.

_____

_____

_____

_____

London in 1601

This city being very large of itself, has very extensive suburbs, and a fort called the Tower, of beautiful structure. [The city] is magnificently ornamented with public buildings and churches, of which there are above one hundred and twenty.

On the south is a bridge [London Bridge] of stone eight hundred feet in length, of wonderful work; it is supported upon twenty piers of square stone, sixty feet high and thirty broad, joined by arches of about twenty feet diameter. The whole is covered on each side with houses so disposed as to have the appearance of a continued street, not at all of a bridge. Upon this is built a tower, on whose top the heads of such as have been executed for high treason are placed on iron spikes: we counted above thirty.

Paulus Jovius, in his description of the most remarkable towns in England, says all are obscured by London... its houses are elegantly built, its churches fine, its towns strong, and its riches and abundance surprising. The wealth of the world is wafted to it by the Thames, swelled by the tide, and navigable to merchant ships through a safe and deep channel for sixty miles, from its mouth to the city. Its banks are everywhere beautified with fine country seats, woods, and farms; below is the royal palace of Greenwich; above, that of Richmond; and between both, on the west of London, rise the noble buildings of Westminster, most remarkable for the courts of justice, the parliament, and St. Peter's Church, enriched with the royal tombs.

This river abounds in swans, swimming in flocks: the sight of them, and their noise, are vastly agreeable to the fleets that meet them in their course. It is joined to the city by a bridge of stone, wonderfully built; is never increased by any rains, rising only with the tide, and is everywhere spread with nets for taking salmon and shad.

Excerpted from *Fragment Regalia* by Sir Robert Naunton

London in 1601 (cont.)

Directions: For each of the details from *London in 1601*, write a brief description (one to three sentences). Write the descriptions in your own words; do not quote from the reading selection.

1. London Bridge _____

_____

2. the towns and landscape below and above London _____

_____

3. The Thames River _____

_____

4. Westminister _____

_____

5. the city of London _____

_____

Directions: Write a short definition of each word, based on what you can tell from the text.

6. extensive _____

_____

7. navigable _____

_____

8. country seats _____

_____

9. shad _____

_____

Camping Cousins

Al was the most amazing person in all of Minneapolis, and he was my cousin. By the age of 19, Al was a star hockey player at the University of Minnesota. He had just earned the rank of Eagle Scout. I wanted to be exactly like him. So when Al asked me to go with him on a spring fishing trip in northern Minnesota, I was elated!

After planning the trip, we gathered gear and supplies, and embarked on our great adventure. We reached the Superior National Forest in northern Minnesota by early evening. We slipped our loaded canoe into the sparkling water and paddled straight to our campsite. We set up camp as the sun was setting, and talked about our plans for fishing the next day.

Al, the former Boy Scout, knew all the tricks of an experienced wilderness camper. After we gathered enough wood from the forest floor, he started the campfire using only flint and steel—no matches. For supper we feasted on freeze-dried buffalo, wild rice, beef jerky, and pea soup. I ate greedily after all that work.

Exhausted, we crawled into our sleeping bags early. Al entertained me with tales of past camping adventures. We were still talking quietly when a sudden north wind picked up, the temperature dropped, and it began to snow. Always alert and innovative, Al found a way to increase the temperature inside the tent. He dragged a log from the woods to the opposite side of the campfire, and laid it across some rocks so it would be off the ground. Then he wrapped aluminum foil around the log. The heat from the fire reflected off the foil and into the tent. Soon images of lake trout were filling my dreams.

The snow had stopped, but sometime later a powerful wind must have kicked up the flames of our dying fire. I was still engrossed in dreams of a 20-pound fish when I was abruptly awakened by Al. A spark had ignited our tent, and flames were engulfing it. Frightened, I bolted out the tent opening. The tent collapsed with Al inside. Without any thought of endangering myself, I reached into the burning tent, grabbed him, and dragged him to the icy lake. We were relieved to find that we were not seriously hurt.

Later, as we stood by the blazing tent to keep warm, we considered our predicament. We were in the middle of nowhere, wearing only underwear, with our supplies grilled into ashes. Even Al was unsure what to do next.

Suddenly, we heard a noise in the forest. Anxiously we listened and stared into the darkness. An all-terrain vehicle appeared on the forest trail. A ranger had spotted the light from the fire and had come to investigate. We jumped into the warm vehicle and the forester drove us to the ranger station, where we were given clothes and were able to call our parents.

Al and I had many more camping adventures, but it was on this trip that Al began to treat me more like a friend and equal, rather than a younger cousin. Our friendship continues to this day.

Name _____ Date _____

Camping Cousins (cont.)

Directions: Complete the story map.

Characters: 1. _____ Setting: 1. Time: _____

2. _____ 2. Place: _____

Events:

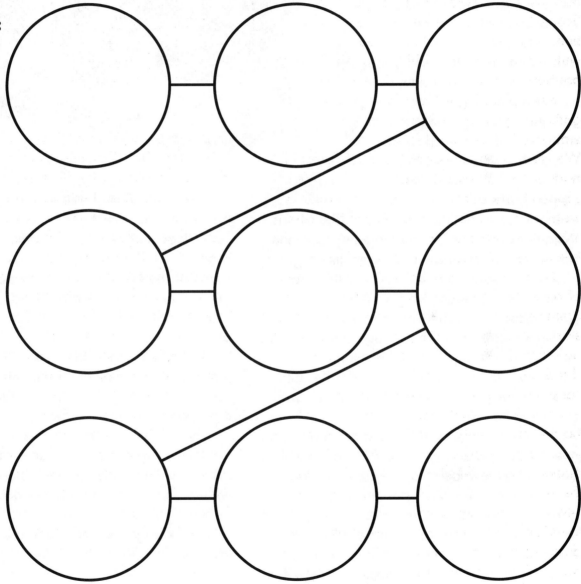

Ending: _____

_____

Visiting Aunt Rita

The landscape changed dramatically as we drove south. The high desert spread out before us as we made our way to Aunt Rita's house. Once or twice a year our family drives out to Aunt Rita's century-old adobe house in a small New Mexico town. We love to visit her and help her with the ongoing restoration of the historic home she bought five years ago. Even though I sometimes dislike doing chores at home, everything seems different at Aunt Rita's house. With her good humor and laughing face, she has a way of making chores seem like a game.

As we drove up to the house, Aunt Rita came out to greet us, a big smile on her face. The reddish-brown house is two stories tall. It has five rooms, including a huge central dining room. We all trooped into that room and sat around the old, planked table while Aunt Rita gave us lunch: a spicy salad topped with cheese and olives.

After lunch, we talked about the chores that needed doing during the week. "Lorenzo will be babysitting the vegetables," Aunt Rita joked. Every time we visit, I am put in charge of the garden. I love working with the growing plants. Depending on the season, I either plant seeds, weed, or harvest vegetables. There isn't much weeding to do, since few weeds survive at this high elevation. Watering, however, is a big job. The water must be hauled from the well, and the plants have to be watered every day. Because I do this work on our visits, Aunt Rita is freed up to work with my parents on bigger repair jobs.

Maggie usually helps to chop and haul firewood. She piles the firewood neatly by the back door and then brings some into the dining room. Aunt Rita uses this wood to keep a fire going in the *kiva*, a special, rounded fireplace in the corner. On this trip, though, she painted a room downstairs that Aunt Rita uses as an office.

My father and mother spend most of their time on these trips helping Aunt Rita with the restoration chores. On this trip, they put new cracked and needed to be replaced.

That night, after an afternoon of work, we made our evening meal. Our favorite dinner is Aunt Rita's homemade vegetable soup, served with tortillas. We sat on the *bancos*, or built-in benches, long after we finished eating. We laughed and joked and made plans to visit our friends in town during the week. Aunt Rita told us the Garcias were planning a cookout to celebrate our visit. Time goes quickly at Aunt Rita's house because we work hard and have such a good time in each other's company.

Visiting Aunt Rita (cont.)

Directions: Circle or write the correct answer.

1. What happens first in the story?

   A. Lorenzo's family eats lunch with Aunt Rita.

   B. Lorenzo's family drives across the high desert.

   C. Lorenzo's family arrives at Aunt Rita's house.

   D. Lorenzo goes to work in the garden.

2. What happens in the middle of this story?

   A. The family eats lunch with Aunt Rita.

   B. The family spends the afternoon working.

   C. The family eats dinner.

   D. The family visits friends.

3. What makes this trip to Aunt Rita's the same as always?

   A. The family will be celebrating a holiday together.

   B. The family will take Aunt Rita visiting.

   C. The family will be helping to repair Aunt Rita's house.

   D. Lorenzo will be chopping and stacking firewood.

4. What makes this trip to Aunt Rita's different than usual?

   A. Lorenzo will be working in the garden.

   B. Maggie will be chopping firewood.

   C. Lorenzo's parents will be helping Aunt Rita with a project.

   D. Maggie will be painting a room.

5. Why does this story seem like part of a larger story?

   A. because we only read about the first day of the visit

   B. because the family arrives to help Aunt Rita with chores

   C. because Lorenzo is unhappy about the visit

   D. because we don't know what Aunt Rita was doing before the family arrived

6. What clues in the story indicate that Aunt Rita's house does not have heat and plumbing?

   _____

   _____

7. Describe Aunt Rita

   _____

   _____

8. Write a short summary of something that might happen on this visit.

   _____

   _____

9. Think of the last time you visited a friend or relative, even for a few hours. Write the beginning, middle, and ending of your visit.

Beginning: _____

Middle: _____

Ending: _____

No Ordinary Storm

From her lifeguard station at the shallow end of the pool, Becky noticed clouds gathering in the sky. By the time she took a break at 2:30, the wind was picking up and the sky was darkening. The pool manager announced over the loudspeaker that the pool was closing immediately, due to a severe weather warning. He asked everyone to head to the safety of home before the storm hit.

All of the swimmers had left by 3:30 except for Jessica's neighbor, eight-year-old Zack Hill. Zack's mother had dropped him off at the pool while she ran several errands. She had planned to pick him up later, but the storm was approaching fast. Jessica decided that she would drop Zack off on her way home. She taped a note for Mrs. Hill on the door of the pool office and headed out.

The minute Jessica and Zack left the parking lot, it was clear that this was no ordinary storm. The wind came in strong blasts, the storm clouds were dense and dark, and the sky had turned an eerie green. The rain hit just as Jessica turned onto her street, coming down in sheets and making it hard to see clearly. Jessica said, "Zack, I'm going to take you to my house. We need to get inside right away, and your house is farther away than mine."

She pressed the garage-door opener, but nothing happened. The electricity was out. The front door was only a few feet away, but the wind was so strong that Jessica and Zack had to fight their way out of the car and into the house. Jessica held Zack's hand firmly. The door was heavy with the pressure of the wind. Finally, it opened, but it was wrenched out of Jessica's hand and it slammed against the side of the house. The window shattered. Jessica picked up Zack and threw the two of them inside; her only thought was to get to a safe place.

Remembering everything she could from her emergency training, Jessica dragged Zack to the basement stairs. Her heart was pounding. The stairwell was pitch black without the overhead light. After what seemed like hours, Jessica felt the door to the storage closet under the stairs. "We'll be safe in here, Zack," she said, trying to sound calm and reassuring. They had just gotten inside when everything went deadly quiet for a moment. Then they could hear the sound of glass breaking and the furniture being tossed against the walls by the wind. A deafening roar, like the sound of a train, filled their ears. "Tuck your head under your arms," Jessica yelled to Zack.

After a final crash, the lifeguard and her charge felt drops of rain on their arms. They saw a flash of lightening through a crack in the ceiling. The sound of the storm grew distant. Jessica began to breathe easier. She and Zack were safe, and what a story they would have to tell!

No Ordinary Storm (cont.)

Directions: Pretend that the questions below are from a newspaper reporter. Write answers for each question as if you were Jessica, the lifeguard from the story.

1. What was your first indication that the storm was going to be a bad one?

   _____

2. Why did you decide to go to your own home instead of Zack's?

   _____

3. What happened when you tried to get indoors?

   _____

4. What did you do once you were inside the house?

   _____

5. At what point were you most worried or frightened?

   _____

6. How could you tell that you and Zack were safe?

   _____

7. What kind of storm do you think you survived? Give examples to support your opinion.

   _____

   _____

   _____

   _____

Newspaper Editorial, 1890

New York City—When I returned from a tour today of the garment sweatshops on the Lower East Side, I vowed that my next editorial would be the start of a great crusade. We must do everything within our power to end this brand of oppression in America. Yes, readers, a kind of slavery still exists! It lives in the tenements of this very city, in crowded rooms and miserable hovels.

Let me take you on a tour of one of the factories I visited. Crammed into two small, dark rooms were no fewer than 20 workers hunched over ever-humming sewing machines. So intent on their work were these human automatons that they did not even notice my presence. They are paid "piece-work," which means that their only hope of staving off starvation is to complete as many sewn pieces as they can. Every finished seam adds a few more pennies to their miserable pay.

One woman paused just long enough to tell me that she never works fewer than 12 hours a day. Her workday begins at dawn and continues until 9 o'clock in the evening. Her pay? Three dollars a week, provided that she works as fast as she can the entire time.

Some of the piece-workers work in their one-room tenement apartments. There, parents and children alike crouch over a single table, sewing by hand to finish garments. Even those who fall ill in the miserable, unheated rooms must keep working, or the family will go hungry.

If a sweatshop worker manages to avoid starvation, he or she may face death from disease. The poor sanitation and lack of heat and ventilation in these factories of misery offer diseases such as tuberculosis an excellent breeding ground.

How can our industry leaders justify the poor pay and working conditions of these and many other sweatshop operations? Why, I have heard them actually say that their work helps keep immigrants out of trouble and children on the straight and narrow path of virtue! Profit blinds these men to seeing justification for the horror that they themselves create.

We must rise up with one voice and say that all people, regardless of their occupation, deserve working conditions and pay that do not put their lives in danger and push their children into early graves. We must find in our hearts the ability to fight for those who are too exhausted, weak, and hungry to fight for themselves. We must do this, regardless of the fight ahead with the richest and most powerful men in this country. I challenge you, readers: speak with a factory owner that you know. Find a community leader to rally groups of people to the fight. Help the poor with your donations. If you do nothing, you will unite yourself with those who keep these miserable workers in the chains of their oppression and poverty.

◆◆◆◆◆◆◆◆◆◆◆◆◆◆◆◆◆◆◆◆◆◆◆◆◆◆◆◆◆◆◆◆◆

Newspaper Editorial, 1890 (cont.)

Directions: Write an answer to each question.

1. Write a summary for this fictitious editorial. What does the writer of the editorial view as the central conflict that he is trying to confront?

   _____

   _____

2. If you were a newspaper reader of 1890, how would you have felt about this editorial? Do you think you would have agreed or disagreed with it?

   _____

   _____

3. What challenge does the writer make at the end of the editorial to his readers?

   _____

   _____

4. What potential conflict could occur if the readers of the editorial take up the writer's challenge?

   _____

   _____

5. What does the writer of the editorial say will happen if the readers do not take up the "challenge" described at the end of the piece?

   _____

   _____

6. Imagine that this editorial was the opening for a longer story. Briefly describe a possible set of characters and a plot for a story about this subject.

   _____

   _____

   _____

   _____

High-Tech Tale

It was the summer of 2020. I was 15 years old, and a computer changed my life. Up until that summer, I had used the computer just like everyone else my age: to link with my instructors, to find film clips and original documents for research, and to keep in touch with my friends around the world. But suddenly, I realized the computer was a magic carpet, a door into any world I wanted to explore. I spent hour after hour on the Internet, going on virtual tours of cities, national parks, and amusement parks. I started e-mailing more and more people and spent whole days keeping up with my correspondence. "Jan, did you ever eat lunch?" my mother would ask. "Have you been outside today? Did you take your sister to that dentist appointment?" Of course, the answer was always no. I hadn't done anything except sit at my computer. I was engrossed by the wealth of information and adventures to be had through its screen.

Then things went from bad to worse. When Jeremy and I took the high-speed train downtown to the library, we missed our stop and ended up two cities away. We got out to take a walk before catching the train back. Around a dark corner under the elevated train tracks, we saw a dingy storefront. It featured a virtual-reality smorgasbord of computer gear and video games. "Come in, come in," said the wraith-like store clerk, who was dressed in floating silk robes. Her voice was silken, too, and hypnotic. Before I knew what I was doing, I had purchased a game called *Mystic Manipulator*. I tucked the package under my arm and we caught the train home.

Within days, I was addicted to my new game. It was a virtual-reality fantasy. My part was as a shapeshifter in a band of adventurers. I could become any creature imaginable, and I was always the hero in every dangerous situation that we encountered. The characters in the game became more real to me than my own friends. In fact, I began refusing calls and e-mails from my friends, and I never went to family meals. I stayed up most of the night because each adventure on *Mystic Manipulator* was more exciting than the last. I didn't want to miss anything.

After a week, my parents burst into my room with an Internet officer, who unplugged my computer right in the middle of a game. I howled with rage as I was taken off to the Center for Online Addiction. But I needed help. I had lost 20 pounds and was suffering from both malnutrition and sleep deprivation. I hadn't bathed in days, my hair was falling out, and I was weak and dizzy. I was put in the hospital wing of the center. Meanwhile, my mother and father packed up my computer and sent it to an elementary school. They also reported the woman who had sold me *Mystic Manipulator* for selling dangerous software to minors. By the end of the summer, I was much better, but was forbidden any computer use for six months. Instead, I was given an ancient machine called a "typewriter" to use for reports and papers.

High-Tech Tale (cont.)

Directions: Circle or write the correct answer.

1. What is the conflict in *High-Tech Tale*?

   A. Jan doesn't want to return to school.

   B. Jan becomes too involved in her research.

   C. Jan spends an unhealthy amount of time on her computer.

   D. Jan and her brother become lost in a strange city.

2. What are the first signs that Jan is spending too much time on her computer?

   A. She e-mails more people and forgets to eat meals.

   B. She buys computer games and spends all her time playing them.

   C. She spends all of her time in chat rooms.

   D. She spends all of her time writing stories and posting them on the Internet.

3. When does Jan's situation get worse?

   A. when she buys new software to create stories and reports

   B. when she buys new software for a virtual-reality game

   C. when she and her brother Jeremy miss their train

   D. when she loses weight and becomes dehydrated

4. How is the conflict in the story resolved?

   A. when Jan's parents bring in an officer to unplug her computer

   B. when Jan throws away her game software

   C. when Jan starts e-mailing her real friends again

   D. when Jan's brother Jeremy talks to her and gets her help

5. What is one detail that shows this story is set in the future?

   A. computer games

   B. an Internet officer

   C. e-mail to friends

   D. classes taken on the computer

6. What kind of help is Jan given?

   A. hospitalization and the removal of her computer

   B. a new diet and the removal of her game software

   C. starting school early and the removal of her computer

   D. going to stay with a different family

7. Write another possible way in which the conflict of this story could have been resolved.

   _____

   _____

   _____

   _____

If You Were Coming in the Fall

If you were coming in the Fall,
I'd brush the Summer by
With half a smile, and half a spurn,
As housewives do a fly.

If I could see you in a year,
I'd wind the months in balls,
And put them each in separate drawers
For fear the numbers fuse.

If only centuries delayed,
I'd count them on my hand,
Subtracting, till my fingers dropped
Into Van Dieman's Land.

If certain, when this life was out
That yours and mine should be,
I'd toss it yonder, like a rind,
And take Eternity.

But now, uncertain of the length
Of this, that is between,
It goads me, like the goblin bee,
That will not state its sting.
                   by Emily Dickinson

If You Were Coming in the Fall (cont.)

Directions: Circle or write the correct answer.

1. What is the main conflict in the poem?

   A. The speaker does not know what day or year it is.

   B. The speaker does not know when she will see her love again.

   C. The speaker is being stung by bees.

   D. The speaker is confused by the passing of time.

2. What does the speaker say is her main worry?

   A. She will count time until her fingers drop off.

   B. She would rather die than not see her love again.

   C. She is "uncertain of the length" of time until she sees her love again.

   D. She is haunted by goblin bees.

3. Which one of these is a metaphor used in the poem? Check the poem for the exact wording.

   A. comparing the summer to a housefly

   B. comparing the months to balls of yarn

   C. comparing death to eternity

   D. comparing a year to a chest of drawers

4. Which one of these is a simile used in the poem? Check the poem for the exact wording.

   A. comparing eternity to the rind of an orange

   B. comparing the summer to a housefly

   C. comparing months to balls of yarn

   D. comparing a year to a chest of drawers

5. Which of these is a good summary of the poem and its conflict?

   A. The speaker could easily cope with the absence of her love if she only knew for how long she had to wait.

   B. The speaker feels stung by the absence of her lover because he never said goodbye.

   C. The speaker misses her love and counts the days until she sees him again.

   D. The speaker is afraid she will never see her love again.

6. This poem speaks to the uncertainty and unsettled feeling of longing for a loved person. What other kind of metaphors or similes could the poet have used to describe this feeling?

   _____

   _____

   _____

   _____

When the Chips Are Down

It fell off again.

"This just won't work, Dexter," Sean said. "The pins are too loose on the chip."

"Maybe we can repair it. We sure can't afford a new chip like that one," replied Sean's friend Dexter.

Dexter's garage felt cooler than the sultry weather outside. The closed-in air held none of the Indian summer heat that would creep under the door or force itself through the thin glass of the window. It was too hot to work. Still, there was only a week and a half before the science fair. The heat was nothing compared to the drive the two students felt to win first place.

Sean tried to reconnect the pin to the computer chip. The soft metal solder slipped into the space near the pin. After it cooled, Sean urged the pins into the motherboard.

"Oh, no! It broke again, Dex. This just isn't going to work," growled Sean.

"What do you think we should do now?" questioned Dexter.

Sean simply shook his head. He knew that there was too little time to get enough money to buy the computer chip they needed to control the robot's "brain." Without that chip, it would be just like any other robot.

"Mom, would you be willing to lend Sean and me some money? We need it to finish our robot for the science fair," Dexter said to his mother as she fixed dinner.

"You know I would help if I could, Honey, but we just don't have the money right now. I'll be happy if I can pay the bills this month," his mother answered.

Dexter called Sean to tell him the bad news. The boys talked and became determined to earn money any way they could. Dexter washed cars for some people up the block. Sean cleaned at his father's shop after the workers left at night. Dexter and Sean both babysat over the weekend, which they really hated. If it meant money for the computer chip, though, they were willing.

They had only two days to go until the science fair. Dexter and Sean slowly counted the money that they had worked so hard to earn. They had $62.30. It was a lot, but not enough for the chip. They were $18.70 short. It was time to tell their science teacher, Mrs. Frommer.

"We tried, Mrs. Frommer, but we just couldn't make enough money for the chip for our robot's brain," the students told her sadly.

Mrs. Frommer smiled. "I have just the thing!" she said. She opened her desk drawer and took out a slip of paper. The boys were ecstatic when they saw it was a 25-percent-off coupon for the local computer store.

When Sean and Dexter stood proudly next to their science fair exhibit, they had a robot that came to life.

When the Chips Are Down (cont.)

Directions: Write the answers to each question.

1. Who are the characters in this story?

   _____

   _____

   _____

2. What is the setting for the story? Name the time of year and specific places mentioned.

   Time of year: _____

   Place #1: _____

   Place #2: _____

   Place #3: _____

   Place #4: _____

3. What is the problem in the story?

   _____

   _____

4. How do the two main characters try to solve the problem?

   _____

   _____

5. What event helps the two main characters resolve their problem?

   _____

   _____

6. Write a brief summary of the story's plot.

   _____

   _____

One Small Light

"Chen! Chen, where are you?" called Lee. Only the October wind called back, its mournful sobbing echoing in Lee's ears. She stood on a slippery rock that jutted up from the black sea. She could not see her brother's fishing boat, and the storm had been raging for nearly an hour. Lee was afraid.

She knew that if Chen could see a light, however small, it would help him guide the boat back toward shore. The young girl had a small oil lamp and two matches she had taken from the boat. She blocked the wind with her body and tried to light the lamp. The first match sparked but then went dark in a gust of wind. Lee took the second match in her shaking fingers. A small flame bloomed. Lee leaned toward the lamp, but a blast of wind stole the tiny flame from her.

Filled with despair, the girl fought back tears. Then she remembered the whistle her father had given her long ago, before he had died. She pulled it from her pocket and put it to her lips. Lee blew with all her might. The shriek of the whistle pushed against the wind. She blew again, and the whistle sounded even louder. But a large wave crashed against the rocks and knocked Lee into the water. She fought her way back to the rock but when she climbed to safety, she found that the whistle was gone.

Lee scanned the horizon desperately. She saw nothing but the storm-tossed waves. As a last resort, she tried calling her brother's name. "Chen!" She waited and strained to hear something, anything, over the wind. "Chen!" Suddenly, Lee felt small and helpless. She sat down on the rock and hid her face in her arms. Her body shook as she cried.

She lifted her head to wipe away her tears, and a small light blinked at her. She stood up and stared, but saw nothing. Then a light out on the sea blinked. The waves rose and fell, and she saw the light again and again. Her heart began to pound with joy. The light was her brother's mast light. His boat had made it through the storm. Lee began to shout again. After a moment, she heard Chen's voice over the noise of the storm. All was well. Chen was headed toward shore.

One Small Light (cont.)

Directions: Complete the story map.

1. Setting

   Time: _____   Place: _____

2. Characters:

   _____

   _____

3. Main Character's Problem:

   _____

4. Events: What happens to keep the main character from getting what she wants?

   First: _____

   Second: _____

   Third: _____

5. Solution: How is the main character's problem solved?

   _____

6. Ending: What is the final scene of the story?

   _____

7. Do you think this story is set in the United States? Why or why not?

   _____

8. Why do you think that Lee is so worried about Chen? Who will take care of Lee if Chen is lost at sea?

   _____

   _____

    © Carson-Dellosa

Titania Arrives at the Bookshop

Titania, a wealthy young woman whose father wants her to have the experience of working at a job, walks to the bookshop, where she meets her new employer, Roger Mifflin.

Titania, after making sure that Edwards was out of sight, turned up Gissing Street with a fluent pace and an observant eye. A small boy cried, "Carry your bag, lady?" and she was about to agree, but then remembered that she was now engaged at ten dollars a week and waved him away....

Roger, who had conceived a notion of some rather peevish foundling of the Ritz-Carlton lobbies and Central Park riding academies, was agreeably amazed by the sweet simplicity of the young lady.

"Is this Mr. Mifflin?" she said, as he advanced all agog from his smoky corner.

"Miss Chapman?" he replied, taking her bag. "Helen!" he called. "Miss Titania is here."

She looked about the somber alcoves of the shop. "I do think it's adorable of you to take me in," she said. "Dad has told me so much about you. He says I'm impossible. I suppose this is the literature he talks about. I want to know all about it. And here's Bock!" she cried. "Dad says he's the greatest dog in the world, named after Botticelli or somebody. I've brought him a present. It's in my bag. Nice old Bocky!"

Bock, who was unaccustomed to spats, was examining them after his own fashion.

"Well, my dear," said Mrs. Mifflin. "We are delighted to see you. I hope you'll be happy with us, but I rather doubt it. Mr. Mifflin is a hard man to get along with."

"Oh, I'm sure of it!" cried Titania. "I mean, I'm sure I shall be happy! You mustn't believe a word of what Dad says about me. I'm crazy about books. I don't see how you can bear to sell them. I brought these violets for you, Mrs. Mifflin."

"How perfectly sweet of you," said Helen, captivated already. "Come along, we'll put them right in water. I'll show you your room."

"Before we begin," said Titania, "just let me give Bock his present." She showed a large package of tissue paper and, unwinding innumerable layers, finally disclosed a stalwart bone. "I was lunching at Sherry's, and I made the head waiter give this to me. He was awfully amused."

"Come along into the kitchen and give it to him," said Helen. "He'll be your friend for life."

Excerpted from *The Haunted Bookshop* by Christopher Morley

Titania Arrives at the Bookshop (cont.)

Directions: Circle or write the correct answer.

1. Who are the characters in this selection?

   A. Mr. Mifflin, Mrs. Mifflin, and Bock

   B. Mr. Mifflin, Mrs. Mifflin, and Titania

   C. Mr. Mifflin, Mrs. Mifflin, Titania, and Bock

   D. Mrs. Mifflin, Titania, and Bock

2. Which one of the characters is not human?

   A. Titania

   B. Mrs. Mifflin

   C. Bock

   D. Mr. Mifflin

3. What indicators does the reader have that Titania is used to a wealthy lifestyle?

   A. She nearly hires a boy to carry her bag and she has dined at an expensive restaurant.

   B. She brings violets for Mrs. Mifflin and a bone for the dog.

   C. She is interested in books and is looking forward to her job.

   D. She is wearing expensive clothing.

4. Why do you think that Titania's father wants her to have a job at the bookshop?

   _____

   _____

   _____

5. When do you think this story might be set? Give reasons for your answer.

   _____

   _____

   _____

   _____

   _____

   _____

6. Based on the dialogue in this excerpt, what kind of personality do you think that Titania has? How do other people react to her? What do you imagine she looks like?

   _____

   _____

   _____

   _____

   _____

7. Write a brief summary of your idea of a plot for this set of characters. What might happen next?

   _____

   _____

   _____

   _____

   _____

A Visit to Green Island

The house was just before us now, on a green level that looked as if a huge hand had scooped it out of the long green field we had been ascending. A little way above, the dark, spruce woods began to climb the top of the hill and cover the seaward slopes of the island. There was just room for the small farm and the forest; we looked down at the fish-house and its rough sheds, and the weirs stretching far out into the water. As we looked upward, the tops of the first came sharp against the blue sky. There was a great stretch of rough pasture-land round the shoulder of the island to the eastward, and here were all the thick-scattered gray rocks that kept their places, and the gray backs of many sheep that forever wandered and fed on the thin sweet pasturage that fringed the ledges and made soft hollows and strips of green turf like growing velvet. The air was very sweet; one could not help wishing to be a citizen of such a complete and tiny continent and home of fisherfolk.

The house was broad and clean, with a roof that looked heavy on its low walls. It was one of the houses that seem firm-rooted in the ground, as if they were two-thirds below the surface, like icebergs. The front door stood hospitably open in expectation of company, and an orderly vine grew at each side; but our path led to the kitchen door at the house-end, and there grew a mass of flowers and greenery, as if they had been swept together by some diligent garden broom into a tangled heap: there were portulacas all along the lower step and straggling off into the grass, and clustering mallows that crept as near as they dared, like poor relations. I saw the bright eyes and brainless little heads of two half-grown chickens who were snuggled down among the mallows as if they had been chased away from the door more than once, and expected to be again.

Excerpted from *The Country of the Pointed Firs* by Sarah Orne Jewett

A Visit to Green Island (cont.)

Directions: Circle or write the correct answer.

1. Which of these is an example of a simile?

   A. the gray backs of many sheep

   B. clustering mallows that crept as near as they dared, like poor relations

   C. the bright eyes and brainless little heads of two half-grown chickens

   D. the tops of the first came sharp against the blue sky

2. Which of these is an example of personification?

   A. strips of green turf like growing velvet

   B. a roof that looked heavy on its low walls

   C. we looked down at the fish-house and its rough sheds

   D. the dark, spruce woods began to climb the top of the hill

3. Which two color words are used more than once in this setting description?

   A. green and blue

   B. blue and gray

   C. green and gray

   D. blue and black

4. If you were not told that this setting was a farm, what clue would indicate that it was?

   A. the vines growing on either side of the door

   B. the fish-house and sheds

   C. the low, clean-looking house

   D. the chickens near the kitchen door

5. What is the author's purpose in the use of the similes, personification, and descriptive adjectives?

   _____

6. Paraphrase a description of this setting. Be sure to use your own words, not the author's.

   _____

© Carson-Dellosa

Answer Key

◆◇◆◇◆◇◆◇◆◇◆◇◆◇◆◇◆◇◆◇◆◇◆◇◆◇◆◇◆◇◆◇◆◇◆

Life in Yakutia .... Pages 4–5

1. B.
2. C.
3. A.
4. D.
5. A.
6. B.
7. C.
8. E.
9. Answers will vary.
10. Answers will vary.

The Indigo Highway .... Pages 6–7

Main: Sea animals use the Gulf Stream current
Supporting: Gulf Stream starts in Florida; Gulf Stream ends in Grand Banks
Main: Gulf Stream is like a river and a barrier
Supporting: moves water faster than any river; pushes warm water toward Europe
Main: Gulf Stream changed travel to Europe
Supporting: called Highway of the Indies; sea captains kept it a secret
Main: Gulf Stream made Pilgrims' voyage difficult
Supporting: voyage lasted 66 days; Gulf Stream pushed Mayflower to Massachusetts
Main: Benjamin Franklin studied Gulf Stream
Supporting: his cousin told him how it slowed the mail; British rejected help from whalers

Dog Data .... Pages 8–9

1. D.
2. C.
3. D.
4. D.
5. A.
6. B.
7. Answers will vary.

Mealtime Manners .... Pages 10–11

1. B.
2. C.
3. B.
4. A.
5. D.
6. A.
7. E.
8. B.
9. C.

Family Tree .... Pages 12–13

1. C.
2. C.
3. D.
4. A.

5. D.
6. A.
7. Answers will vary.

Pirates .... Pages 14–15

1. E.
2. C.
3. A.
4. B.
5. F.
6. D.
7. a person who is punished for the actions of others
8. Answers will vary.

Mathew Brady's Career .... Pages 16–17

1. B.
2. A.
3. D.
4. B.
5. Answers will vary, but should include a reference to this being the first modern media coverage of a war.
6. Answers will vary.
7. Answers will vary.

Alex in Charge .... Pages 18–19

1. F
2. T
3. F
4. F
5. F
6. T
7. Answers will vary.
8. Answers will vary.

The Irish Famine .... Pages 20–21

1. B.
2. E.
3. A.
4. C.
5. D.
6. F.
7. Answers will vary, but should present a concise summary of the main facts.

Mummies Have No Secrets .... Pages 22–23

1. No
2. Yes
3. Yes
4. No
5. Yes
6. Yes

Answer Key

◆◆◆◆◆◆◆◆◆◆◆◆◆◆◆◆◆◆◆◆◆◆◆◆◆◆◆◆◆◆◆◆◆

Canoes .... **Pages 24–25**

Venn diagram should be filled in correctly.
Dugout: burned to make; paddled by two people; used by the Arawak; made from a tree
Both: types of canoes; waterproof; stable water transportation
Kayak: made from a wood or bone frame; paddled by one person; used by the Inuit

Vampires? .... **Pages 26–27**

Vampires Column: Gender, male; Appearance, pale, staring eyes; Behavior, bite others, sleep during day; Death, can rise up after death
Rabies Victims Column: Gender, mostly male; Appearance, spasms, tired; Behavior, bite others, wander at night; Death, look lifelike after death

At Sheila's House .... **Pages 28–29**

1. B.
2. A.
3. C.
4. B.
5. D.
6. Answers will vary.

Prairie Pioneers .... **Pages 30–31**

Chart should be filled in correctly, based on general knowledge of domestic dogs.
1. Answers will vary, but should include differences between wildlife and domestic animals; habitat differences; the fact that prairie dogs are not actually members of the dog family, etc.
2. Answers will vary, but should include the fact that wolves and other wild dogs are carnivores and hunt other animals for food; that wolves do not build community structures, etc.
3. Answers will vary, but should include the community nature of the prairie dogs' lives; their social structure such as living in coteries and having guards; their ability to build homes that protect them from being prey, etc.

Amber .... **Pages 32–33**

1. F
2. F
3. O
4. F
5. O
6. F
7. F
8. F

9. O
10. O
11. Answers will vary.

A Letter to Camilla .... **Pages 34–35**

1. F
2. O
3. F
4. O
5. O
6. F
7. O
8. O
9. F
10. Answers will vary.

Tramp Art .... **Pages 36–37**

1. During the Depression, many people were unable to find jobs.
2. Tramps left their homes to look for work.
3. Tramp art is a folk art from Europe.
4. Some tramp art had intricate geometrical designs.
5. Tramps were impoverished and had to scavenge materials.
6. This art is considered valuable today.
Wording of answers will vary.

Northern Lights .... **Pages 38–39**

1. the aurora borealis
2. omen
3. the Inuit belief about the aurora borealis
4. people in 16th century France
5. the aurora borealis
6. a cloud of particles
7. the aurora borealis
8. communications systems
9. weather reports or newscasts
10. the aurora borealis
11. Answers will vary.

Remarkable Rooms .... **Pages 40–41**

1. Jules' Underwater Lodge
2. pizza
3. Ariau Jungle Hotel
4. Ariau Jungle Hotel
5. monkeys
6. rooms in a Japanese capsule hotel
7. beds in the Ice Hotel
8. Ice Hotel
9. Ice Hotel dining room
10. Answers will vary.

Answer Key

Walls of Water .... Pages 42–43

1. X
2. S
3. S
4. X
5. X
6. S
7. S
8. S
9. X
10. S
11. Answers will vary.

The Birthday .... Pages 44–45

1. M
2. S
3. S
4. M
5. S
6. M
7. S
8. M
9. The cake was a sweet dream of chocolate.
10. The gifts were boxes of delight.
11. The games were bursts of noise and excitement.
12. The guests were like a community of friends.
13. The dog was like a detective, tracking down cake crumbs.
14. The house was like a bright flower with its colorful decorations.
15. Her skin was peaches and cream.
16. His smile was a beacon of light.
17. The cat was a jungle animal as it stalked the mouse.

Rhyme Schemes .... Page 46

1. E.
2. A.
3. D.
4. B.
5. C.

Ballad of a Cherry Pie .... Page 47

1. B.
2. D.
3. B.
4. A.
5. Answers will vary.

The Bee Is Not Afraid of Me .... Page 48

1. B.
2. A.
3. D.
4. A.
5. Answers will vary.

Three Haiku by Bashō .... Page 49

1. B.
2. C.
3. B.
4. A.
5. Answers will vary.

Ode to Autumn .... Page 50

1. B.
2. A.
3. B.
4. Answers will vary, but should be appropriate to one specific season.

Pebble Rings, Like Memories .... Page 51

1. It expresses grief for something lost or dead.
2. like the song that each of my memories sings
3. ring/sings (or any ending from a couplet pair)
4. an older (middle-aged to elderly) man
5. sad for the death of his son and his lost youth
   Wording of answers will vary.

The Eagle .... Page 52

1. Answers will vary but should indicate a description of an eagle.
2. like a thunderbolt, he falls
3. the sky
4. a lyric poem, because it is musical and expresses an image from nature
5. aaa/bbb

We Crouch in Caves .... Page 53

1. Answers will vary but should indicate it is about a father and child working in a coal mine.
2. This place is an endless ebony tunnel.
3. Answers will vary but should indicate that the miners are longing to be elsewhere or lost in other thoughts as they work.
4. a father and his child
5. Answers will vary; this poem can have several interpretations as to tone.

Ozymandias .... Page 54

1. A.
2. C.
3. A.
4. C.

Food for Thought .... Page 55

1. D.
2. F.
3. H.

4. A.
5. G.
6. B.
7. C.
8. E.
9. I.

The Good Bacteria .... Pages 56–57

1. B.
2. C.
3. A.
4. C.
5. D.
6. C.
7. A.
8. C.
9. B.
10. Answers will vary.

Leonardo's Way of Seeing .... Page 58

1. A.
2. A.
3. B.
4. B.
5. A.
6. B.
7. B.
8. A.

Analogies .... Page 59

1. D.
2. B.
3. A.
4. B.
5. D.
6. A.
7. A.
8. D.

Survival .... Pages 60–61

1. C.
2. B.
3. A.
4. B.
5. B.
6. A.
7. C.
8. D.
9. B.
10. Answers will vary.

Time for Lunch .... Page 62

1. B.
2. C.

3. A.
4. B.
5. D.
6. B.
7. D.
8. C.
9. A.

Recipe for Success .... Page 63

1. C.
2. B.
3. B.
4. A.
5. D.
6. B.
7. A.
8. B.
9. A.

The Amazing Amadeus .... Pages 64–65

1. B.
2. B.
3. C.
4. C.
5. B.
6. B.
7. Answers will vary, but should include main points from the selection.

A Soldier with a Secret .... Pages 66–67

1. No
2. No
3. No
4. Yes
5. Yes
6. No
7. Answers will vary, but should include the main events of Wakeman's life.

A Hidden Wonder .... Pages 68–69

1. It is biography; it is not written by Jim White and it is written in third person.
2. In 1901, I saw a large, black cloud as it poured out of the earth.
3. Autobiography is written by the subject of the work him- or herself.
4. Ray V. Davis bravely toured the caves to capture their beauty on film. (Example)
5. Order of events: 4,3,1,2,5,7,6

Answer Key

◆◆◆◆◆◆◆◆◆◆◆◆◆◆◆◆◆◆◆◆◆◆◆◆◆◆◆◆◆◆◆◆◆◆◆◆◆◆◆

The Young Life of Frederick Douglass................
.... Pages 70–71

1. autobiography
2. cabin
3. ladder
4. slave
5. Old Master
6. free
7. grandchildren
8. born
9. 1817
10. first
11. Answers will vary.

When Lightning Strikes .... Pages 72–73

1. Answers will vary but should indicate that the article is about lightning: what it is and how it effects people.
2. students, science fans, or people interested in weather facts
3. because Franklin is a familiar historical personage and creates an instant mental image
4. Yes. Examples will vary.
5. to tie the conclusion back to the introduction, which features Benjamin Franklin and his kite
6. to inform; to educate readers so they can use the safety tips themselves
7. 1 in 2.5 million
8. to inform

Golden Words .... Pages 74–75

1. Examples: devious, exiled, drum up, used her charm, treacherous
2. to imply that she was improper, a risk-taker, or both
3. It implies that her death was a punishment for her political views.
4. Answers will vary.
5. Answers will vary.

Doctor Anna .... Pages 76–77

1. determined
2. energetic, pioneer, curiosity, or determination
3. The author implies this was unfair to women; the specific sentence is, "No school could limit her curiosity or her determination."
4. It was worse in the summer and fell off after the frost killed the plants.
5. the author's
6. Answers will vary, but should include the main facts of Doctor Anna's life.

Contemplating Color .... Pages 78–79

1. blue, calm, to feel cool
2. red, love/passion, to increase heart rate
3. green, nature/healing, to decorate hospital rooms

4. black, death/evil, mourning clothes
5. purple, royalty, to stimulate creativity and intuition
6. Answers will vary.
7. Answers will vary.
8. Answers will vary.
9. Answers will vary.

Lincoln's Dream .... Pages 80–81

1. B.
2. A.
3. B.
4. D.
5. B.
6. Answers will vary.

Dick Turpin's Ride .... Pages 82–83

1. B.
2. C.
3. D.
4. C.
5. B.
6. C.

Venice... Pages 84–85

1. A.
2. A.
3. B.
4. A.
5. C.
6. B.
7. A.
8. C.
9. Answers will vary.

The Baseball Card .... Pages 86–87

1. C.
2. omniscient; the reader "hears" both characters' thoughts.
3. B.
4. A.
5. Answers will vary, but could include knowledgeable, honest
6. Answers will vary, but could include financially needy, worried, grateful (at the end)
7. You would not know the value of the card or anything about the difficulty of Mark's decision. You would also not know how much the seller of the card needed the money or why.

A Letter Home................................. Pages 88–89

1. from the point of view of the letter writer, a young soldier; first person
2. young, opinionated, lonely (reasons will vary)
3. He says they fought bravely and calls them heroic.

◆◆◆

4. He calls them turncoats and says Lenin has things "under his thumb."
5. Answers will vary.

In Another Country .... Pages 90–91

1. Answers will vary, but could include sensitive, caring, decent.
2. He is troubled by the plight of the poor.
3. Answers will vary.
4. The poor wait outside the restaurant, hoping for food.
5. Answers will vary.

Geraldo's Journal .... Pages 92–93

1. Answers will vary, but could include fearful, experienced seaman, religious, worried.
2. sea monsters and that his ship will sail off the edge of the world
3. From the names of the ships, it is clear that this is Columbus' expedition of 1492.
4. They were signs that land was nearby; the wood had not been in the water long and the birds needed to rest on land at night.
5. Answers will vary, but should include factual information about Columbus' expedition.
6. Answers will vary.

The Dinner Party .... Pages 94–95

Possible information could include:
Personality: simple, modest, amusing
Childhood Memories: raising turkeys, skating and rescuing boy from drowning
Favorite Meal: bread and milk
Home: Euclid Avenue mansion (Cleveland, Ohio)
Social Status: millionaire, richest man in the world

Vacation .... Pages 96–97

1. classroom and speaker's home
2. Answers will vary, but should include specific information from the story.
3. December
4. Answers will vary. The speaker does mention some specific outdoor activities.
5. Chart answers will vary. Some possible answers include: Sight, gray clouds and brown-tiled lobby; Sound, rustling of wrapping paper and shrill bell; Taste, salty pretzels and tart punch; Smell, scent of vanilla and scent of almonds; Touch, silky scarf and cold windowpane

In the Village .... Pages 98–99

1. sight; small, brown, grass-roofed
2. sight; huge, snow-capped
3. touch; cold
4. hearing; barking, braying

5. touch; rough and dry grass
6. smell (or taste), spicy
7. sight; distant, terraced
8. smell; strong, bitter
9. hearing; distant cries
10. sight; red-gold embers
11. Answers will vary.

London in 1601 .... Pages 100–101

1.–5. Answers will vary, but should include specific details from the text.
6. abundant, widespread
7. able to allow ships to travel on it
8. country manors or estates
9. a kind of fish

Camping Cousins .... Pages 102–103

Characters: 1. Al
                2. his cousin (the speaker)
Setting: 1. probably early spring
                2. northern Minnesota
Story Map: events should be written in chronological order
Ending: The cousins are rescued by a ranger; they have many camping adventures afterward.

Visiting Aunt Rita .... Pages 104–105

1. B.
2. B.
3. C.
4. D.
5. A.
6. Firewood heats the dining room; water for the garden comes from a well.
7. Answers will vary; examples are hardworking, good-humored, fun to visit.
8. Answers will vary; students might mention visiting the neighbors, the cookout, house projects being completed or challenges associated with them.
9. Answers will vary.

No Ordinary Storm .... Pages 106–107

1. I knew there was a bad storm coming when the pool was closed due to severe weather warnings.
2. My home was closer and we needed to get indoors quickly.
3. The garage-door opener didn't work so we struggled to the front door. The wind blew it out of my hand and broke the glass.
4. We headed straight for the basement. The lights were out and it was difficult to find our way.
5. I was most frightened when the house was destroyed above us.
6. The noise quieted; the storm sounded as if it had

passed.

7. I think the storm was a tornado. There was a green sky, high winds, and the wind sounded like a freight train. The storm also did a lot more damage than an ordinary thunderstorm.

Newspaper Editorial, 1890 .... Pages 108–109

1. Answers will vary, but should include information about the treatment of factory workers.
2. Answers will vary.
3. He asks the readers to speak with factory owners, start rallies or ask others to do so, donate money, and anything else they can think of to correct the injustices he has described.
4. The factory owners would fight back and things might get worse.
5. If readers do nothing, they unite themselves with the despots who run the factories.
6. Answers will vary.

High-Tech Tale .... Pages 110–111

1. C.
2. A.
3. B.
4. A.
5. B.
6. A.
7. Answers will vary.

If You Were Coming in the Fall .. Pages 112–113

1. B.
2. C.
3. B.
4. B.
5. A.
6. Answers will vary.

When the Chips Are Down .... Pages 114–115

1. Dexter, Sean, Dexter's mother, Mrs. Frommer
2. Fall (Indian summer); garage, Dexter's kitchen, classroom, science fair
3. The boys need a new computer chip but don't have enough money to buy one.
4. making money by cleaning, washing cars, babysitting
5. Mrs. Frommer gives them a computer-store coupon.
6. Answers will vary.

One Small Light .... Pages 116–117

1. Time: at night; Place; the sea coast
2. Characters: Lee and her brother Chen
3. A fisherman's young sister fears that he has been lost in a storm.
4. She tries to light a lamp for Chen, but the wind blows out her matches. She then blows a whistle, but loses it

in the sea. She calls out her brother's name over the wind.
5. She sees a light on the horizon.
6. Lee hears Chen calling to her.
7. This story could be set in the United States or in an Asian country. There is nothing to indicate what language is being spoken, the specific location, or any cultural context clues other than the Asian names of the two characters.
8. It is implied that Lee has no family except Chen. They might be orphans.

Titania Arrives at the Bookshop.... Pages 118–119

1. C.
2. C.
3. A.
4. He may want her to experience middle-class life. (In fact, in the novel, it is revealed that Titania's father is afraid she is too privileged and snobbish, and he wants to help her change her attitudes.)
5. Titania's language is dated. She is also wearing spats. (The novel is set in 1919.)
6. She is friendly, outgoing, and well-mannered. Both Mr. and Mrs. Mifflin are immediately charmed by her. She is probably nice-looking.
7. Answers will vary.

A Visit to Green Island................ Pages 120–121

1. B.
2. D.
3. C.
4. D.
5. to create a strong visual picture of the setting
6. Answers will vary but should include specific details from the description.